IAN AL

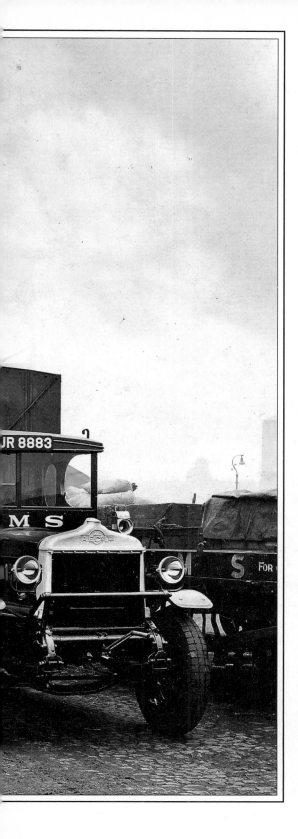

IAN ALLAN TRANSPORT
LIBRARY

ALAN TOWNSIN

Ian Allan
PUBLISHING

Front cover:
This 1937 AEC Regent is representative of London Transport's STL class of the mid to late 1930s, the backbone of that fleet until supplanted by the RT in postwar years. STL2093, which has bodywork built in 1939 at LT's Chiswick works, was restored by D. J. Cowing and is seen at Brighton on an Historic Commercial Vehicle Society run — it is nowadays owned by the London Bus Preservation Trust. *Geoff Lumb*

Back cover (upper):
AEC pioneered the rigid eight-wheeler. This petrol-engined Mammoth Major of type 680 was built in September 1934 for J. M. Mills Ltd of Liverpool. Nowadays owned by the Science Museum, it is seen at Wroughton in 1989 after a superb restoration supervised by Harry Pick, President of the AEC Society. *Author*

Back cover (lower):
The AEC factory built 8,821 of the Y-type models, mainly for use by the Army, in the latter part of World War 1. The chassis of this example with Tyler engine dates from 1917. It was discovered derelict in the 1960s and restored by Jack Henley in 1970, being seen at the 1992 AEC Society Rally. *Author*

Title page:
Vehicle life expectancies were often very low in the earlier days of road transport — frequently around seven years or so. Rugged military vehicles helped to show that this need not be so. This Y-type lorry run by the LMS Railway bears a 1931 registration number, evidently issued after a thorough rebuild, yet is of the type AEC was building towards the end of World War 1. It was being used to demonstrate the procedure for transferring early-style containers from road to rail using a Walker Bros mobile crane. *Ian Allan Library*

First published 1998

ISBN 0 7110 2620 3

Published by Ian Allan Publishing

an imprint of Ian Allan Publishing Ltd, Terminal House, Station Approach, Shepperton, Surrey TW17 8AS. Printed by Ian Allan Printing Ltd, Riverdene Business Park, Molesey Road, Hersham, Surrey, England.

Code: 9810/B

Below:
Portugal was a very important market for AEC vehicles and after production at Southall ceased, the UTIC concern continued to assemble vehicles incorporating AEC units for several years. Rodoviaria Nacional was formed in the late 1970s as a nationalised concern rather on the lines of the National Bus Company and as late as 1991 was operating 1,915 AEC or UTIC-AEC vehicles out of a total fleet of 3,022 buses and coaches. This example was seen in Sintra in 1982. *David Studdard*

Contents

Acknowledgements

It would be impossible to list all the many people who have contributed to my almost lifelong study of AEC, which began with schoolboy journeys in petrol-engined Regent buses in 1936 and included a fascinating spell in the drawing office at Southall in 1951-5. An interview in 1964 with G. J. Rackham, who had retired in 1950 after 22 years as AEC's Chief Engineer, still ranks among the most fruitful of my later career as a writer — how I wish I could have asked him more.

More specifically regarding this volume, I must thank Gavin Martin and Brian Thackray, both AEC experts of long standing, for responding to various queries as well as reading the draft text, leading to some useful clarifications and improvements. Acknowledgement is also due to the British Commercial Vehicle Museum Trust archive, in which Gordon Baron has done stalwart work in preserving and sorting AEC material in particular. Others who helped in various ways include Brian Goulding, Philip Groves, Tim Nicholson and Harry Pick.

The illustrations come largely from the Ian Allan Library or my own collection, both including many of AEC origin issued for publicity purposes. Other pictures are as acknowledged individually, though I would like to thank the Omnibus Society, the Imperial War Museum and the London Transport Museum for their co-operation.

Introduction

AEC's existence as a vehicle maker lasted for 67 years, ending nearly 20 years ago, yet its importance seems to be better understood today than then. The AEC Society must surely be the strongest of all the one-make commercial vehicle clubs and the number of preserved AECs steadily grows — there are surprising numbers still in normal use.

AEC's origin as the chassis builder for the London General Omnibus Co Ltd, and the continuing close liaison with London Transport up to the mid-1960s, had a strong influence on its character. Close links of this kind between suppliers and customers are apt to be frowned upon nowadays, yet AEC's awareness of the realities of running a big fleet of vehicles benefited all its customers.

Its innovative ideas, sometimes fostered by the aim that London buses should be 'the best', were widely copied. Ease of maintenance was a priority and hence characteristic of most of AEC's best known products, whether passenger, goods or military.

Yet not everything went smoothly — now and then, AEC paid the price of pioneering with spells of difficulty. At times, the sheer torrent of fresh products meant that not all were fault-free, yet most of the best known were remarkably sound, as preserved examples often testify.

The link with Leyland made in 1962 as a means of better tackling foreign competition in export markets is still a matter of controversy — AEC's role soon began to diminish, if at first only gradually, even though vehicles worthy of the name were being built to the end.

Could AEC have survived had it remained independent? Probably not in today's world of international mergers, although the success of Dennis does sometimes make one wonder. Perhaps a more pertinent question is whether Leyland as a high-grade commercial vehicle group might have survived had it avoided links with already-flawed big-volume car manufacturers.

What is beyond question is the sheer inventiveness of AEC's engineers and its influence on commercial vehicle history, as I hope this volume will help to indicate.

Alan Townsin
Steventon, Hants
August 1998

Left:
This Renown six-wheeler, built in the autumn of 1931 for the London General Omnibus Co, was fitted with a 60-seat body built by LGOC as a prototype for 1932 production. These photographs were taken to show the improved destination display added before it entered service in January 1932. At that stage LT741 had a petrol engine but it was used for a further development exercise later in 1932 when it was fitted with a Gardner 6LW engine as part of the major pioneering study of diesel power units undertaken by LGOC and AEC, mainly involving the latter's own engines. *LT/Ian Allan Library*

1. A Healthy Inheritance

The Associated Equipment Co Ltd, later to become far better known as AEC, was registered on 13 June 1912, and could be said to have hit the ground running. It took over what was already a busy bus chassis manufacturing factory at Walthamstow on the eastern outskirts of London, previously run by the firm which was to be by far its largest regular customer for the next 21 years, the London General Omnibus Co Ltd.

The LGOC had been set up in 1855 to amalgamate horsebus-operating concerns in London and 50 years later its fleet of such vehicles had reached a peak of over 1,400, by far the largest in the capital. The motorbus first appeared on the London scene at the turn of the century, initially in various small-scale ventures, mostly so unreliable as to be soon abandoned. Yet by 1905 it had been developed to the stage of becoming a serious threat to the horsebus. Several concerns were competing for business, inducing the LGOC to put sizeable numbers of its own motorbuses into service.

Three years later, on 1 July 1908, a merger brought together the LGOC and its two largest motorbus-operating competitors. The larger, with 386 vehicles, then the biggest motorbus fleet in London, was the London Motor Omnibus Co Ltd, using the fleetname 'Vanguard' and the Walthamstow works which were to become the original home of AEC were inherited from that concern, the original modest premises having been built in 1906.

Up to then, most of the buses operated in London were on imported chassis. Among the best known were the Milnes-Daimler — which used chassis from the German Daimler company better known in Britain by the Mercedes name by then being used for its cars — and the French De Dion. Vanguard had set up a subsidiary, Motor Omnibus Construction Ltd, using the Walthamstow works to assemble units made to its designs. These were made largely by Armstrong Whitworth, a large engineering firm based in Newcastle upon Tyne, though they also supplied complete some identical chassis — the engines were made by Richard Hornsby & Sons of Grantham. About 20 were produced for Vanguard and the associated Pilot fleet in 1906-8, though a few others were also sold elsewhere.

Meanwhile, in 1907, the LGOC had appointed Frank Searle as its Chief Motor Engineer. He had joined the company earlier that year as garage superintendent at Mortlake and his initial training in steam locomotive work had instilled the orderly ways of the Great Western Railway into the LGOC, bringing a sense of order to the previously somewhat chaotic maintenance methods. Soon after the 1908 merger, he put forward a scheme for the LGOC to design and manufacture its own bus chassis at the ex-Vanguard Walthamstow premises.

Below:
By 1905, the London General Omnibus Co Ltd had had 50 years of experience in running a large fleet of horse-drawn buses, its final standard 26-seat design being a model of light yet sturdy construction. The motorbus pioneers were handicapped by management steeped in the world of horses but the body design expertise was to prove useful. *AEC/Author's collection*

This was agreed and thus the LGOC X-type was born, using a combination of the features found most satisfactory in the combined fleet. As was usual at the time, it was of what was called 'normal-control' layout, with the driving position behind the front-mounted four-cylinder petrol engine and a relatively high straight frame, much as used on goods vehicles. On this was mounted bodywork of similar open-top double-deck layout to that of the final type of horsebus, though rather larger and seating 34 passengers. An example of the adoption of ideas from existing buses was the choice of the sandwich frame as favoured by De Dion, basically wooden but flitched with steel reinforcing plates, this having been found less prone to the cracking experienced with early steel frames.

Regulations governing the size and weight of London buses were particularly tight, length then being limited to 23ft, width 7ft 2in and unladen weight 3 tons 10cwt. In those days, these and other matters (notably noise) were controlled by the Metropolitan Police, and the X was at first judged unsatisfactory with regard to the noise from its gearbox, which was typical of that era in having straight-cut spur gears. This led to the adoption of what was called a chain gearbox, using sets of sprocket wheels and chains in place of gears, which became a regular feature of buses for the LGOC until the late 1920s. Fortunately, the worm-drive rear axle proved acceptably quiet. A total of 61 X-type chassis were built in 1909-10, one being used as a lorry.

While the X was in production, its far more famous successor, the B-type, was being designed. Though very similar-looking, again with 34-seat open-top body as standard, the design was much improved. The engine, a four-cylinder unit as virtually universal in those days and with the T-head layout then common, initially of 110mm bore, 140mm stroke and 5.3-litre capacity, was quoted as giving a modest 30bhp, though reputedly much livelier than the X of nominally similar output. From 1913, an increase in bore to 115mm gave 5.8 litres and 36bhp — contemporary accounts indicate little more sound than a faint carburettor hiss up to 10mph or so, the rumble from

the solid tyres being the most prominent noise — officially, speed was limited to 12mph.

More importantly, and aided by the methodical maintenance methods, the B was a reliable vehicle, helping the LGOC to replace the horsebuses and greatly expand its network. Delivery of chassis began in October 1910, by which date 250 had been ordered, followed at intervals by further similar batches, and a year later the last LGOC horsebus was taken off the road.

Such events doubtless helped to draw the attention of the Underground Electric Railways Co of London Ltd, by then already running much of the tube network as still existing today. The outcome was the takeover of the LGOC by the Underground group. A key figure in AEC's history was Albert Stanley, already Managing Director of UERL, who took office in the same role for LGOC from April 1912. He was created Lord Ashfield in 1920, for many years being not only the dominant figure with regard to public transport in London but also playing a key and direct role in the creation of AEC and the guidance of its fortunes until 1933.

The expansion of bus operation in London had also made other British manufacturers aware of the possibilities. Leyland, still a modest-sized firm but beginning to grow, had backed a London-based operator from 1906.

Above:
When AEC came into being in June 1912 to take over the LGOC's chassis-manufacturing activities, the output of the B-type, which had been in large-scale production since October 1910, rose to 30 per week for a time. It enabled the LGOC to expand its network of routes, stretching into quite rural areas, as shown in this view of B2325, which was typical of the production examples being produced in 1913. As well as being reliable, it is said to have been noticeably livelier than the X-type. *AEC/Ian Allan Library*

Above right and right:
The B-type chassis was simple in most respects but sound in design, with ease of maintenance particularly in mind, this last becoming an AEC tradition. These views also show the inlet and exhaust sides of the four-cylinder engine and the mid-chassis positioning of the chain gearbox. The serial number B2567 was both the chassis and operator's fleet number. *AEC/Ian Allan Library*

This threat had faded but a more serious one came from the Coventry-based Daimler Co Ltd, which had long since lost even the initial tenuous connection with the German company from which it took its name. By then Daimler was well established as a maker of high-quality cars but its management had been persuaded of the potential of the bus, and proposed a London bus venture.

By May 1911, the LGOC board, having heard a rumour that Frank Searle had been invited to run this Daimler bus project, sacked him as Chief Engineer after he had refused to accept the terms of a new five-year contract to stay with

them, and he duly joined Daimler, designing a bus visually very similar to the B-type, save for the radiator outline with a locally domed portion under the filler cap. It used a four-cylinder (110mm x 150mm) 5.7-litre 40hp Daimler engine having the sleeve valves by then favoured by that firm on the grounds of quiet running. The British Electric Traction Co Ltd, then owning a chain of tramway companies including two major ones in London, became involved, forming a company to run a fleet of Daimler buses in London.

Against this background, almost the first step taken by

Above:
Although intended as a bus chassis, the B-type was also used when the LGOC had need of a commercial vehicle — this sturdy-looking but narrow van body on B2480 was used by the commercial advertising department. The standard radiator had small LGOC lettering, as seen here. *AEC/Ian Allan Library*

the Underground group with regard to the LGOC was to separate its chassis manufacturing facility, creating the Associated Equipment Co Ltd as a wholly-owned UERL subsidiary in June 1912. It was not the most exciting of names, and with its existing function confined to supplying another Underground subsidiary, few could have foreseen how widely the initials AEC would become known.

The fact that Albert Stanley was appointed Managing Director of AEC was no mere formality and a further significant appointment to the new company was that of Walter James Iden, another railway-trained engineer who had been Works Manager at Walthamstow since joining the LGOC from Crossley in 1909. He immediately aided Searle in the design of the B-type engine and succeeded him as Chief Engineer to the LGOC from 1911. On AEC's creation, he combined this post with acting as Chief Engineer and General Manager to the new company.

From the beginning, the concept of AEC as a manufacturer trading on the open market rather than continuing merely as supplier to LGOC was intended. In the event, freedom of action was somewhat limited for some time by the outcome of negotiations with regard to BET's activities in London and Daimler's plans. These eventually led, among other things, to a five-year agreement that Daimler would act as sole selling agents for AEC chassis sold outside the Underground group. Thus began what was to be a long and complex intermittent relationship with Daimler.

More immediately, output at Walthamstow, organised by Iden, was increased to 30 per week for a time and some 2,682 B-type chassis had been built by the end of January 1914. At that period this was an almost unprecedented rate of production in Britain, certainly for a commercial vehicle, and it seems unlikely that any other motor factory in the country — except for Ford's then new plant at Trafford Park, Manchester devoted to the much smaller model T car — was regularly building one type at such a rate.

The standard 34-seat bodywork, much as used on the X-type, was generally built in the LGOC's body workshops in Holloway, although some bodies were contracted to outside bodybuilders. Most were finished in the LGOC's red livery, although some were painted in the colours of various other concerns as part of the complex agreements reached in the process of expansion of the bus network. AEC did not become involved in body manufacture either for vehicles built for the LGOC or, in due course, other customers. This continued to be the case in later years, although AEC did sometimes provide body or cab designs.

Sales of B-types outside London up to 1914 were very small. The first such customer was United Automobile Services Ltd of Lowestoft, a fast expanding operator, which received six special long-wheelbase B-type double-deckers in 1913, this sale being negotiated before the agreement with Daimler was in effect. They bore the full Associated Equipment Co title on the radiator, unlike most chassis built for LGOC which generally continued to have the style used in pre-AEC days, bearing the LGOC initials in small lettering. About eight more B-type chassis to LGOC specification were sold to 'outside' customers under the agreement with Daimler (including the first three exports, to New Zealand) before the outbreak of World War 1.

203

Above:
A venture by the Daimler Co Ltd to become involved in the manufacture of buses for use in London led to an invitation to Frank Searle to take charge of the project. The result was a bus of similar general appearance to the B-type but with a Daimler sleeve-valve engine and a radiator of distinctive shape. Subsequent negotiation led to Daimler being appointed as selling agents for chassis made by AEC except for those built for the Underground group.
AEC/Author's collection

Right:
In September 1913, the first of 30 chassis for the LGOC was completed to a new design, with pressed-steel frame and 14ft wheelbase; there were similarities to the 3-ton Daimler B-type chassis then being developed for more general sale. It seems that the police were not willing to approve the type for use as a double-decker and hence they were completed as 20-seat single-deckers. The radiator of this first such bus, B2679, though of standard LGOC B-type pattern, carried 'A.E.Co.' lettering in the form of intertwined initials but the remainder had radiators more in Daimler style. After the outbreak of war in August 1914, they became ambulances for the War Department. *AEC/Ian Allan Library*

2. Wartime Turns AEC into a Lorry Maker

The sales agreement with Daimler barely had time to produce commercial returns before the activities of AEC became completely altered following the outbreak of war in August 1914. In July 1913, the last of the main run of buses for the LGOC, B2678, had been exhibited by Daimler at the Commercial Vehicle Show held at Olympia. Significantly, it had a Daimler 40hp engine of

5.7-litre swept volume, as had been used for the Daimler CC model designed by Frank Searle.

It was considered that, for more general sale, somewhat heavier-duty chassis than the B as built for the LGOC were needed. Prototypes in 3-, 4- and 5-ton form with chassis derived from the standard B, but with Daimler 40hp engines, were built at Walthamstow early in 1914,

Right:
Almost as soon as war was declared, orders at the Walthamstow factory greatly increased to meet the War Office demand for vehicles, which meant that the factory had to be enlarged. By 25 January 1915, the framework for two large four-storey machine shops was nearing completion.
AEC/Author's collection

Below:
Compulsory takeover of civilian vehicles for military use began immediately after war broke out in August 1914. The LGOC had 1,185 of its buses taken for such duty and soon many of them were operating in France or Belgium. In this scene, dated 6 November 1914, the 2nd Battalion of the Warwickshire Regiment is being carried in a convoy of B-type buses in Dickebusch *en route* for Ypres, already the scene of major battles. Note that B2067, leading the convoy, has its canvas weather protection for the driver carefully labelled with its civilian fleet number. *Imperial War Museum*

these models being known as the Daimler B. A four-speed conventional spur gearbox was designed for them, although the three-speed chain gearbox was optional for the 3-ton model and was fitted to most of the early examples. The 3-ton version was slightly more substantial than the LGOC B, the others more obviously so.

Daimler ordered production batches from AEC, mainly of the 3-ton model, and modest numbers were delivered to operators during the spring and summer of 1914, including buses for municipal and other fleets. Some were described by operators as Daimler CC-types, perhaps having been ordered as such; outwardly, they were of similar appearance.

However, on the outbreak of war, in addition to compulsory acquisition of many existing buses, including some 1,185 from the LGOC, all new production was diverted to the War Office. Thereafter, apart from rare

exceptions, output went to the military, mainly the Army, until the end of the war in 1918.

Output of new chassis had slackened in the previous year as the LGOC's immediate needs had been fulfilled, but now the War Office was keen to see production increased. Authorisation for building new four-storey machine shops and extending the site followed within a few weeks. Outstanding orders for LGOC-type B-type chassis that had been deferred were put in hand, but for military use.

Once regular output for the War Office became established, the 3-ton Daimler B was revised in specification, with spur gearbox for all production, heavier-duty springs and wheels. This version became known as the 3-ton W model — altogether, some 481 of the Daimler B and W were built in 1914-15, the chassis numbers of these and later types until the early 1920s continuing in the same numerical series as earlier LGOC B-type chassis, though generally omitting the prefix. Most of the military chassis had the characteristic Army-style lorry body with canvas tilt — the cab was also canvas topped. In February 1915, a new X-type designation was used by Daimler for an interim development of the W, with heavier-duty rear hubs, 140 being built.

The Y-type designation dated from March 1915; it

applied to what was initially a further minor revision from the X-type, lower-geared and with a modified clutch stop. Some 2,799 such chassis were built in just over two years, and the Y-type and its later derivatives were to become the best known of all the wartime variants. Small numbers of new Daimler Y-type chassis were released to some municipal transport undertakings in 1915-16 for the transport of war workers.

Initially, it was planned that new bus chassis would be built for the LGOC and others as replacements for those taken for war service in 1914. Material for these was ordered but some of it was used to build 3-ton chassis for the Russian Government in 1916-17, others being diverted elsewhere. From a design viewpoint they were regarded as Type Z, but in some production records they were listed as 'Russian B'. Another more rare designation was the S-type, applied to 10 4-ton and 10 5-ton chassis originally ordered by Daimler in 1914 but built in 1916, and incorporating the Y-type rear axle.

From the end of June 1916, the Walthamstow factory came under direct government control, and chassis were no longer supplied via Daimler. As the five-year agreement expired in December 1917, it was agreed that it would be allowed to lapse. AEC thus again traded under its own name, beginning to display its initials on the radiator in an Underground-style bull's-eye motif, though the humped shape of the top tank introduced by Daimler continued, this combination remaining standard into the 1920s.

Further extensions to the factory were completed in 1917, including a new assembly shop with a moving conveyor line, thought to be the first for a British heavy-duty commercial vehicle maker. Output rose from the 30 chassis per week that had been normal in 1916 to 45 per week by the end of 1917.

By January 1917, the model sequence had advanced to Type YA, which used a proprietary Tylor JB4 engine, itself built to a War Office specification, again with four cylinders but now with side valves (in early days called 'side-by-side' to indicate they were all on the same side of the engine instead of the T arrangement previously used). The 5in bore and 6in stroke meant that its swept volume was some 7.7 litres, a capacity which by coincidence was to become familiar on a much later AEC engine. At first the Tylor engines in chassis bearing the 'AECoLtd' name were intermingled on the production line with Daimler units in chassis bearing the Daimler script, but later they became standard.

Then the YB appeared, based on the YA but with a pressed-steel frame, while Type YC had a David Brown final-drive worm-gear unit. A new War Department contract for 4,750 YB and YC chassis placed that year was subsequently increased to cover 7,750 chassis. By March 1918, output was up to 20 chassis per day.

When hostilities ceased in November 1918, the total of Tylor-engined YA, YB and YC-types had reached 5,200, outnumbering all other models built at Walthamstow up to then. By that date, the factory space amounted to 483,000sq ft as compared to the 3,000sq ft of the original Vanguard premises in 1906, and 2,800 people were employed. Deliveries to the War Office continued until July 1919, by which date 6,022 had been delivered. The combined total of Daimler and AEC Y-type variants was thus 8,821.

Weekly output of up to 130 chassis was mentioned in some subsequent reports of AEC's wartime efforts, which quoted a total of 10,000 military 3-4-ton models, representing 40% of the total of all makes in this category supplied during the war period.

Even allowing for an element of convenient rounding of the figures, AEC had become a very capable large-scale maker of heavy-duty commercial vehicles. Inevitably, cancellation of military contracts soon brought a halt to such production rates but, initially, the level of demand meant that much of the material that had been ordered was used to meet civilian orders for Y-types, selling briskly through 1919. The total sanction of 7,750 Tylor-engined chassis ran until about 1922, but latterly many were completed with AEC 5-type engines, becoming Type 501 or 505.

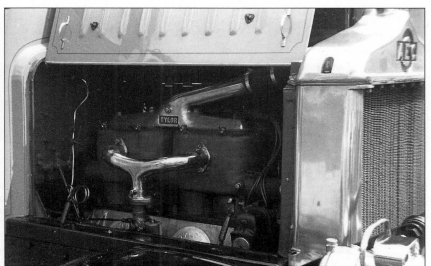

3. The Competitive 1920s

Although demand for new vehicles had been brisk just after the 1914-18 war, a harsher climate soon emerged. A problem faced by AEC and other firms that had made rugged military vehicles in huge numbers during the war was that many of them became surplus when it ended and were sold off. Even if rather battered-looking as bought, many were restored to roadworthy condition for a total cost far below that of new examples, of which sales dropped sharply for several years. Moreover, by 1922 Britain was in a trade depression, reducing the amount of business on offer and sharpening competition.

Fortunately, the LGOC needed large numbers of new buses and was able to adopt a more radical approach in regard to their design, keeping AEC quite busy through a difficult time. A final batch of 250 B-types was built in 1919 but a fresh initiative led to the introduction of the K-type, of which the prototype entered service in August that year.

Its main new feature was forward-control layout. Seating the driver over the engine had been quite widely used in Edwardian times but made maintenance more difficult. The Scottish Motor Traction Co's Lothian bus of 1913 had the driving position alongside the engine, inside a full-fronted cab. The K can be credited with combining this idea with good engine accessibility by establishing the half-cab concept, so characteristic of buses in most major fleets in Britain for the next 30-40 years.

This, and the use of transverse seats in the lower deck, enabled the seating capacity to be increased from the 34 of the B-type to 46 while keeping within the 23ft-length limit. Yet the claimed 'dry' unladen weight of the complete bus as first developed was kept down to 3 tons 8cwt. The side-valve four-cylinder 100mm x 140mm engine was smaller than that of the B-type at 4.4 litres, this being given the type number A101 in a new unit numbering system that was to become characteristic of the marque. Similarly the gearbox, again of the chain type, began a fresh series at D101; the rear axle, of the underslung-worm type, was F101 and so on. By the end of 1921, deliveries to the LGOC fleet had reached K1077, to which were added small numbers built for use elsewhere and others completed later — some were built as single-deckers and others rebodied thus.

Below:
A final batch of 250 B-type chassis for the LGOC were built from December 1918 to April 1919, B5033 and B5028 leading this line-up. The radiator had acquired the hump-topped outline as first used by Daimler but destined to remain AEC's standard until the mid-1920s, the bull's-eye motif bearing the word 'General' on those for the LGOC. *AEC/Ian Allan Library*

Meanwhile, experiments with larger buses had led to the introduction of the S-type, the first entering service at the end of 1920 as the restrictions on London bus dimensions had been eased to permit length of up to 25ft and unladen weight to 5 tons. In production form as built from late 1921, the S gave a seating capacity of 54 in an enlarged design of similar layout to the K, using the first of a series of 108mm x 140mm four-cylinder engines of 5.1-litre capacity used in a variety of AEC models in the 1920s, the initial version being of type A107.

The S was still a very simple design of bus, with straight flitched frame, unassisted brakes on the rear wheels only and open top but it set a pattern for the size of two-axle double-deckers in Britain that was to be exceeded only slightly over the following 35 years — indeed, it was some years before buses of so large a capacity became common outside London. The LGOC placed 895 S-type buses in service during the period up to late 1923, some assembled by the operator. Others were supplied to municipal and other company fleets but only in modest numbers.

AEC adopted a three-digit model numbering system using series based broadly on the nominal load capacity of the respective ranges. Thus the K-type, regarded as a 3-ton model, began at 301, the 302 being a version as supplied outside the LGOC; the standard London S-type began what was often called the 4-type series at 401.

A new AEC four-cylinder side-valve engine of 120mm bore, 150mm stroke and 6.8-litre capacity had been developed to replace the Tylor unit of the later Y-types. This change created the 501 bonneted model, intended mainly for goods work and in production from late 1921 to 1926 — a longer wheelbase version was later added as the 505, occasionally fitted with passenger bodywork. The 501-type chassis were numbered 501001 upwards, this classified method of chassis numbering becoming usual for AEC models built for general sale, though for several years those for the LGOC continued to use a series which had begun at 20001 with the first K prototype and not altering with changes of model.

By contrast, Types 502 and 503, introduced in 1923, were forward-control passenger chassis based on the S-type, complete with flitched frame but with the larger 5-type engine and a conventional four-speed sliding-mesh gearbox. Some were supplied for operation in country areas around London by LGOC associates, being given numbers in a PS series signifying 'Provincial S', and for 30 years or more the word 'provincial' in AEC-speak continued to mean a vehicle intended for an operator outside London and sometimes of different design accordingly.

As military production ceased, AEC was able to offer rapid delivery of new chassis and this example of a Y-type was one of a batch of nine supplied to the Great Western Railway and fitted with charabanc bodywork built in the railway workshops. No 196 was first licensed in July 1919, though the Carmarthenshire registration was a reissue from an earlier vehicle. The standard radiator by that stage carried plain AEC lettering rather than the 'AECoLtd' version used on earlier examples. *AEC/Ian Allan Library*

Other provincial operators favoured the smaller engine, some taking the 401 model as built for LGOC with three-speed chain gearbox, and others the 403, introduced in 1922 with conventional gearbox. Type 404 was a bonneted left-hand-drive export version of which a single example was built for Toronto.

Below:
An indication of fresh thinking after the return of peace was the introduction late in 1919 of the K-type with its half-cab forward-control layout, setting the standard in front-end layout for British double-deckers for the next half-century. Most of the type were built for the LGOC but this was one of six supplied to the East Surrey Traction Co Ltd, in 1920. *AEC/Ian Allan Library*

Sales of these provincial models were relatively modest, though some names which were to prove important to AEC began to appear in the order lists in 1922-3, notably Birmingham Corporation and South Wales Transport Co Ltd, both of which took S-type models, initially with the smaller 4-type engine but later adopting the 5-type and converting earlier vehicles.

The idea of enclosing the upper deck of double-deckers had obvious appeal in Britain's uncertain climate and had been common practice on trams since Edwardian times. Yet there was nervousness on the stability implications for a motorbus, not least on the part of the ever-cautious Metropolitan Police, and it was primarily to ensure stability that a new lower-built chassis was designed. This was the NS, derived from the S-type but with a pressed-steel frame having a lowered centre section and even lower tail, the latter allowing the entrance platform to be

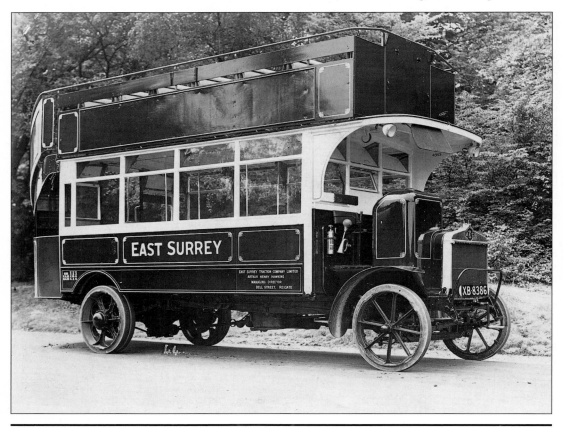

EAST SURREY

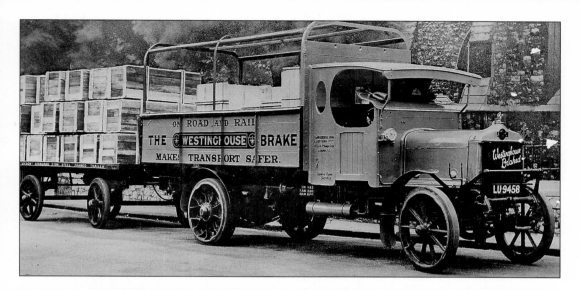

only one step up from the ground and requiring one further step to enter the lower saloon.

The key mechanical feature permitting this was the rear axle, which had a dropped centre section driving the rear wheels via an internally-toothed gear attached to the brake drum assembly. A similar mechanism had been used on Milnes-Daimler buses but not exploiting the possibility of lowering height, which had been taken up in some American designs. However, the design of the NS is generally credited to Charles K. Edwards, who had been promoted to Chief Draughtsman of AEC in 1916 — the post of Chief Engineer had been allowed to remain vacant but Edwards was the firm's senior engineer of that period.

The first NS chassis were built in December 1922, but the police rejected the closed-top body design and the type was put into production with open-top bodywork. This

Top:
The possibilities of increased load capacity by towing a trailer had obvious appeal. The lettering 'Westinghouse Braked' on the radiator of this Y-type outfit was an example of shrewd advertising, the Westinghouse Brake & Saxby Signal Co Ltd already being well known on railways, and parts of what may have been an early air-pressure system are visible. Yet smooth-surfaced solid tyres and the absence of brakes on the front wheels gave limited scope for effective brake action on lorries of that period. *AEC/Ian Allan Library*

Above:
Some K-types were bodied as single-deckers, both for use by the LGOC and elsewhere, this one being of a style perhaps intended to appeal to municipal operators. Note how the LGOC-style driver's cowl was extended upwards by a windscreen. *AEC/Ian Allan Library*

continued until a further experiment with four covered-top buses, NS1734-7, in late 1925, following which permission was granted for general use, including the conversion of the existing NS buses.

Initial NS chassis were of type 405, with one of AEC's very rare instances of a gearbox using helical gears, again with three speeds. This was evidently troublesome and was dropped in favour of a reversion to chain gearboxes of different types on the 407 and 408, the latter version retained for subsequent NS deliveries. The LGOC had opened a spacious new central overhaul works at Chiswick in 1921 and for a period from late 1924, NS and

other chassis were assembled there from parts supplied by AEC.

The initial rebuff to LGOC's venture in adopting a top-covered double-decker delayed the introduction of a provincial NS, but Birmingham Corporation interest led to the development of an S-type with wider track — type 504 — fitted with covered-top body of which the first was completed in June 1924. In all, 108 of the type were added to that fleet in the period up to 1926.

A provincial version of the NS, the 409, appeared at the beginning of 1925, and ironically a complete top-covered bus was exported to the agents in Buenos Aires before any

Left:
The first S-type appeared in November 1920, initially seating 57 passengers and even though this was reduced to 54 before entry into service with the LGOC, it must have seemed a big bus when the 34-seat B-type was still the main type on London's streets. Although simple and spartan by later standards, it set a standard for size and seating capacity that was only slightly exceeded by the majority of British double-deckers up to the mid-1950s. It went into production in 1921 as AEC's model 401, S30 being seen here.
AEC/Author's collection

Below left:
The 503 was one of a family of models derived from the S-type, the first digit indicating that it had the 5-type 6.8-litre engine rather than the 4-type 5.1 litre, though both were four-cylinder petrol units. This 1924 example for W. Jellie of Lisburn was used on a service to Belfast and had 36-seat bodywork by Strachan & Brown. *AEC/Author's collection*

Below:
The 201 2-ton model represented an attempt to bring AEC into a higher-volume market, using an engine of very simple design, with a two-bearing crankshaft and one-piece cast-iron cylinder block and crankcase. This 1924 example had bodywork by E. & H. Hora Ltd and was photographed at Walthamstow. *AEC/Ian Allan Library*

Bottom:
The heaviest AEC model of its day was the solitary 7-type, numbered 701001 — an 8/10-ton articulated six-wheeler with hefty 9.7-litre four-cylinder petrol engine, built in 1923. The front end of the semi-trailer was carried on a turntable directly mounted on the springs of the driving axle. It is shown in this publicity picture with a van body, the latter possibly no more than an artist's impression. It did not find a buyer until 1926 when sold to Cory Bros of London, the trailer then having a tanker body.
Ian Allan Library

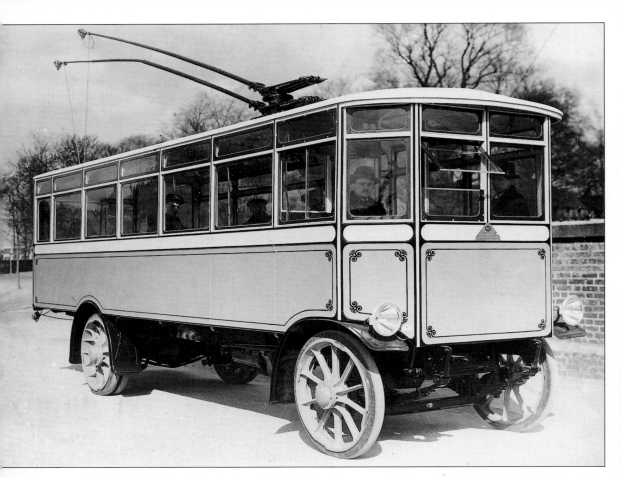

AEC added trolleybuses to its range of products in 1922. What is thought to have been the first to be built was this 602-type with 36-seat body, sent for experimental operation to the Mexborough & Swinton Tramways Co in March 1922. The chassis was derived from the S-type bus model.
AEC/Author's collection

The NS-type was designed with the aim of introducing covered-top buses in London but the Metropolitan Police refused to approve the prototype in this form and it was put into production in 1923 for the LGOC as an open-top bus, though with lower build and a single-step rear platform giving it a clear advantage over the previous S-type. A few were built for other operators, this being chassis number 408002 supplied to Hull & District Motor Services Ltd in September 1924. In August 1926, when Hull & District was incorporated into the newly formed East Yorkshire Motor Services Ltd, it was sold to the LGOC and taken into stock as NS1953.
AEC/Author's collection

entered service in London. A dispute with the German electrical concern AEG led to an agreement that AEC products for South America and Germany bore the name ACLO (signifying 'Associated Company's Lorries and Omnibuses'), this vehicle being among the first such. An order for 41 of the 409 resulted from Anglo-Argentine Tramways later in the year, but these were bodied as single-deckers and had pneumatic tyres. Eight open-toppers went to the East Surrey fleet; in 1926 10 with covered tops were supplied to Waterloo & Crosby Motor Services Ltd and small numbers went to other operators.

After further tests in autumn 1925, existing NS buses in the LGOC fleet were fitted with covered tops, two examples dating from 1923 seen here being refuelled in the newly opened Elmers End garage in 1929. The petrol tank on early forward-control AEC buses was mounted immediately behind the bonnet.
Ian Allan Library

H. Kerr Thomas, who had been Works Manager of the American maker Pierce Arrow, was appointed Resident Director of AEC in 1920 and it was his idea that AEC should build a 2-tonner, introduced at the 1923 Commercial Show. The design was aimed at low cost — its 4.4-litre engine had the same bore and stroke as that in the K-type, but was of much simpler design with combined cylinder block and crankcase. The main types were the 201 goods version with solid tyres, and the 202 with pneumatics and longer wheelbase for use as a small bus. Although eventually 917 were built, that total was not reached until 1928 and the volume never built up to the level needed to make such a venture effective.

At the other end of the weight scale was the 7-type, an articulated six-wheeler built in 1923 and evidently a reaction to Scammell's success with a vehicle of this type. It had an engine of no less than 9.7-litre capacity, yet still four-cylinder, and a form of air-pressure braking, but only one example was built.

Trolleybus production began in 1922 with a series of models numbered 601 upwards, mostly single-deck and built in small numbers. The most significant was the 603, which had a set-back front axle permitting the entrance to be in the front overhang, in the manner nowadays familiar but then very rare. An initial fleet of 100 chassis was built to the requirements of the Shanghai Electric Construction

Co in 1924, said to be the largest trolleybus order ever built at the time. The model remained in production until 1939, latterly as the 603T, and a total of 282 were built, largely for Shanghai.

A significant development in March 1925 was the introduction of a light bus chassis intended to seat about 30 passengers in forward-control form. This was type 411, intended to meet a proposed 3 tons 15cwt weight limit for models with pneumatic tyres if they were to be permitted to run at 20mph instead of 12mph. It used an improved version of the 5.1-litre 4-type engine and was basically simple but the introduction of pneumatics to a 'full-sized' bus was a major step forward. For the first time, model names were used by AEC, the 411 being called Renown and the equivalent 412, Blenheim; these were followed later in the year by the 413 and 414 with modified brake systems, still acting only on the rear wheels. A total of 405 of the two forward-control types, and smaller numbers of the bonneted versions, were built for a variety of operators, some quite small.

Two further named models were the 506 Grenville and 507 Ramillies introduced in the autumn of 1925, respectively a bonneted model mainly for goods use and a forward-control type for passenger or goods duty — both had pressed-steel frames and brought AEC's flitched-frame era to an end.

Left:
By 1925, pneumatic tyres became available for medium-sized vehicles and this 505 for the Busy Bee fleet of Richards of Caernarvon thus fitted is seen before delivery — the 32-seat body was by Strachan & Brown. The four-storey workshops of AEC's Walthamstow works visible in the background were not ideal for the manufacture of commercial vehicles and the management was considering a move to a more suitable site.
AEC/Author's collection

Above:
Solid tyres persisted longer on double-deckers than smaller vehicles and this demonstrator, built to a design developed for Birmingham Corporation in 1924, was briefly numbered 15 in the Glasgow Corporation fleet and registered GB 6914 in that city. It had a Short Bros body and is shown at Walthamstow with 'Model 4' labels in the windows but was recorded later as a type 504, so may have switched from a 4-type to a 5-type engine. It was not purchased by Glasgow and was added to the Sheffield Corporation fleet in February 1926.
AEC/Author's collection

Above:
The first AEC Renown model was a light single-decker, the example shown being one of 10 model 413 buses with Short Bros 30-seat bodywork for Sheffield Corporation supplied in 1926. *Short Bros/Author's collection*

Below:
Model names, mostly associated with the Royal Navy, were favoured briefly by AEC in the mid-1920s. This was a Grenville, model 506, a new 5-ton bonneted type intended mainly to carry goods introduced in the latter part of 1925. It had a pressed-steel frame and the radiator had a slightly slimmer casing than on previous models, though overall it was clearly still in the Y-type tradition. *Ian Allan Library*

4. Associated Daimler

There was unease about the future of AEC in 1925. A drop in LGOC's need for new buses was foreseen when NS deliveries were completed, with the prospect of almost all the fleet dating from 1920 or later. Moreover, the fact that the NS chassis assembly was in hand at Chiswick drew attention to the LGOC's increasing capability to go its own way. The limited scale of other business obtained by AEC was also worrying, though exports were growing. Furthermore, the Walthamstow works was no longer thought satisfactory for modern needs and a move to a new site was proposed.

Another strand to the atmosphere of change arose from an approach from the Daimler Co Ltd later that year. This revived the idea of co-operation on bus and lorry sales,

this time as a joint organisation and involving the use of recently designed Daimler six-cylinder engines offering the prospect of greater refinement. (That company continued to have immense prestige as a maker of high-grade cars, not least for the Royal Family.) On the other hand its Coventry-built bonneted 2/3-ton goods and bus

Below:
The formation of Associated Daimler was the signal for what would nowadays be called a rebranding operation. The new 416 model single-decker had a radiator with the name spelled out across the top tank and the new company initials 'ADC' applied to the filler cap. This example with a full-fronted 32-seat body by Short Bros was supplied to J. Hennessy of Cork in the spring of 1927. *AEC/Author's collection*

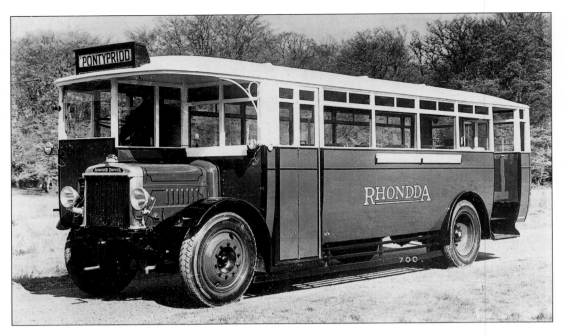

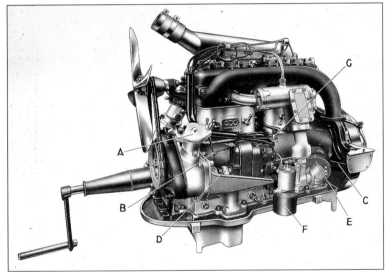

Above:
The Rhondda Tramways Co Ltd took delivery of four buses with bodywork by Hall Lewis on ADC 415A chassis early in 1927. The 415 had been produced as an AEC type since April 1926, meeting a United Automobile Services Ltd need for a model longer than the 413 and with a shorter cab, made possible by the removal of the petrol tank from the position behind the bonnet hitherto favoured because of Metropolitan Police preference. Few were supplied to other users, the Rhondda examples being among the last built. *AEC/Author's collection*

Left:
The 4-type 5.1-litre engine in the A119 form offered in the 416A as introduced was typical of commercial vehicle petrol engines of the mid-1920s in being a side-valve four-cylinder unit and having a modest output of 45bhp — note that it carried ADC lettering on the tappet covers. It was perhaps a little dated even in 1927 in relying on what was called splash lubrication and retaining a fixed cylinder head, but proved reliable. *AEC/Author's collection*

Right:
On paper far more advanced, Daimler's sleeve-valve six-cylinder engine had full-pressure lubrication and was supposed to develop up to 70bhp despite a smaller swept volume of 3.568 litres. One is seen here set at the angle of the bus installation. In practice, the CV25 version used by ADC proved disastrously unreliable when used on bus work and many such engines were replaced by 'old-fashioned' 4-type units. *AEC/Author's collection*

chassis of basically pre-1914 design, still offered up to 1924, had latterly found few buyers.

Lord Ashfield was in favour of both these proposals. By the beginning of 1926, a new factory site had been found adjoining the Great Western Railway main line at Southall, on the western outskirts of London, and construction work began.

Negotiations with Daimler took a little longer but the Associated Daimler Co Ltd was set up on 25 June 1926. The plan was for it to be equally owned by AEC and Daimler though the two firms acted rather cautiously from the outset by simply sharing costs, with no set date for share issue. ADC was to be responsible for choosing the

Above:
The development of pneumatic tyres had reached the stage of allowing their use on double-deckers during 1926. Some early examples were on six-wheel (three-axle) models, but the first on an NS, and among the first on any make of two-axle double-decker, was this 409-type bus for Greyhound Motors Ltd of Bristol which entered service early in 1927. Its Short Bros 52-seat body was largely to LGOC specification. The rear wheels had to retain the large diameter dictated by the NS axle but at the front a 36x8 size was used, much the same as the 9.00-20 found on many buses still in service today. *AEC/Author's collection*

models to be offered and their design as well as sales, AEC and Daimler undertaking manufacture.

Lord Ashfield became Chairman of ADC and another eminent name involved was that of Laurence Pomeroy, appointed as Chief Engineer. However, his duties in the same position with Daimler at Coventry, where he had recently arrived after a spell in America, again meant that Charles Edwards's role as Chief Designer, initially still based at Walthamstow, was more important than it appeared.

The new AEC factory at Southall also housed ADC's administrative and sales offices, the basic idea being that AEC would make the chassis, and it was intended that, from 1927, Daimler would supply most of the engines for ADC vehicles. For the time being, manufacture of complete AEC-designed vehicles would continue, initially at Walthamstow. Production of Daimler cars and AEC manufacture for the LGOC were not affected by the ADC enterprise.

In practice, the initial effect was largely one of badge engineering. Lettering reading 'Associated Daimler' or 'ADC' replaced AEC on radiators, hub caps and even engines of AEC design, though Daimler engines were always described as such.

A model already in production as an AEC from April 1926 which was a pointer to later developments was the 415, basically a longer version of the 413 and built to the

requirements of United Automobile Services Ltd which was fast expanding its services in East Anglia and the northeast of England. Shareholdings in that company were taken up by nominees of the LGOC, some held from 1920 but on a larger scale in 1926-7, building up to over a quarter of the issued capital. This was not revealed publicly, perhaps because there was an agreement with BET that LGOC would not operate beyond 30 miles of Charing Cross, but on the other hand, the purpose seems to have been purely to help United buy the large numbers of buses it needed, thereby boosting AEC/ADC output, with no attempt to interfere in UAS management. The effect was much as offered later by finance companies — there was also similar support for the Glasgow Omnibus Co and the Belfast Omnibus Co. The first 100 AEC 415 buses for the United fleet went into production in the spring of 1926, being followed by 140 ADC 415s in 1927.

During 1925-6, pneumatic tyres had become usual for single-deckers generally and there was a growing demand for such vehicles. Accordingly, the first new models publicised by ADC were the forward-control 416 and bonneted 417, having the same 16ft wheelbase as the 415

but with a frame cranked downwards slightly between the axles and at the rear, as had become accepted practice on passenger models, to allow a lower floor line. By this time, four-wheel brakes were becoming more common and were available as an option, as was a vacuum servo.

The 416 and 417 were offered with a choice of the 4-type 108mm x 140mm four-cylinder engine of AEC design, by then type A119 and developing 45bhp, or a Daimler six-cylinder sleeve-valve engine. This was sometimes confusingly described at the time as the 40/70hp unit but more precisely defined as type CV25, which indicated its derivation from a 25hp Daimler car engine introduced in 1924, with 81.5mm bore, 114mm stroke and 3.568-litre capacity and running at up to 3,000rpm, at which the 70bhp implied in its designation was claimed. The chassis types were given suffix letters 'A' or 'D' according to the engine fitted, this also applying to other models including the 415 — some of the 1927 batch were 415Ds.

The first chassis built in the new Southall works in February 1927 were 416A models, the supply of Daimler engines not allowing the 416D to follow until later. As it turned out, this was something of a blessing in disguise, for the CV25 engine intended as the key feature of the new range was to prove disastrously troublesome. The problem lay in its lubrication system, which though on paper thoroughly up-to-date as a full pressure system, was inadequate for the hard work demanded from a bus engine and led to repeated seizures and big-end failures. Before long, teams of engineers were struggling to keep buses on the road, changing engines and repairing those removed so as to deal with others as they failed. The old-fashioned-seeming splash-lubricated 4-type engine produced a tortoise and hare effect, proving far more reliable within its more modest capabilities.

Hence, contrary to intentions, the 4-type engine was kept in production for 1928, and indeed improved to Type A127 with detachable cylinder heads. Most 416 models had 4-type engines from new and quite a number of others were converted to them — overall, some 987 of the type were sold in 1927-8, mostly to provincial company and municipal operators, with 124 of the bonneted 417, making the pair the largest-selling single-deckers built by

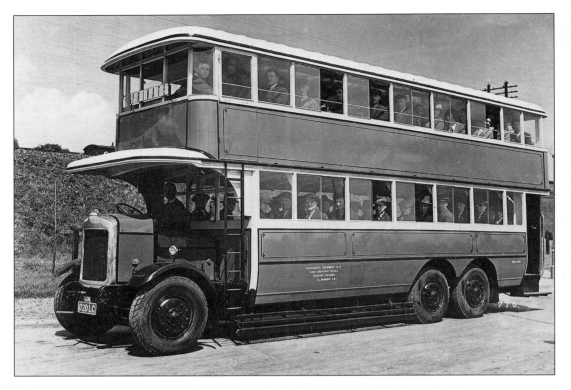

Right:
The 507 introduced as an AEC model in 1925 continued through the ADC era, being taken up by Birmingham Corporation as its standard type in the 1927-8 period. This example for Bassett's of Gorseinon is seen at Southall in the summer of 1928, by which date ADC was falling apart. This was one of the last chassis of this type numerically, with chassis number 507238, though Birmingham continued to put examples into service into 1929. *AEC/Author's collection*

AEC/ADC up to then. Model 418 was a bonneted 3½-ton goods model with a front end like the 417, and 375 were built, continuing until 1931.

The type number 419 was given to a special coach model, based on the 416D but with special front end and radiator, 33 being built for the LGOC plus six for East Surrey. They were outwardly similar to eight coaches derived from NS chassis that had been built at Chiswick in 1926. All had canvas-topped 'all-weather' bodywork.

There was strong interest at that time in rigid six-wheeled (three-axle) vehicles. Initially, this was related to the use of pneumatic tyres, another concept first pursued in America. In Britain the introduction of buses of this layout by Karrier and Guy in 1925-6, with sales to quite a number of municipal fleets, prompted ADC to follow suit —

indeed two planned new two-axle double-deckers were abandoned in favour of the 802, also known by its LGOC type code LS, signifying 'London Six'. This was designed at Walthamstow, having a conventional four-speed gearbox and a rear bogie having two worm-drive axles driven via a third differential to balance the torque between them. This had been patented by Charles Edwards and AEC in August 1926 to eliminate a source of failures on existing six-wheelers. Rod brakes were fitted on the bogie wheels only, though air-pressure operation, then very rare on motor vehicles, was fitted to some later 802s.

The first example, LS1, 29ft 1½in long and seating 68 passengers but still only 7ft 2in wide, entered service with LGOC in June 1927 — its LGOC body had enclosed stairs as built. A new AEC-built 7.6-litre detachable-head side-valve 108mm x 140mm six-cylinder engine, Type A121, had been designed for the model but this was not ready and a Daimler CV35 sleeve-valve unit was fitted. This was derived from the 35/120 car engine, of 97mm bore, 130mm stroke and 5.7-litre capacity. The next two chassis had the A121 engine, one being a works bus used to carry workers from Walthamstow to the new Southall works and the other the second LS.

Another works bus and six chassis for use as demonstrators made up the first 10, these having the CV35 engine which became standard for the model. Some buses for public use seated up to 72 — the works buses seated 104 and 102 respectively, using gangway seats, not

Left:
Seen here when new, the second 802-model bus was completed in July 1927 to carry AEC employees from Walthamstow area to the new works at Southall, a journey of over 16 miles across London. The LGOC-built body seated 104, using folding seats in the gangways — some press reports called it 'the world's largest bus'. In December 1928, a prototype AEC oil engine was fitted, allowing the claim to be made that this was the first diesel bus in London, and probably in Britain, even though not in public service. *AEC/Author's collection*

Below:
The LGOC reverted to the NS in July-August 1928, when 50 on the 422-type chassis with pneumatic tyres entered service, including NS2300 seen here. This required permission to exceed the width limit of 7ft 2in previously enforced but advantage was then taken of the new 7ft 6in width to redesign the body with drop-type opening windows. A final six similar buses were delivered in May 1929. *AEC/Ian Allan Library*

permissible on a public bus in Britain. Pomeroy did not favour the A121 engine, so only two more of these chassis received them, being included in 10 more LS-class buses built for the LGOC in 1928. On paper the 802 model was fully comparable to six-wheelers offered by other makers at the time but no orders outside LGOC came in.

Meanwhile, the existing 409 version of the NS and the 506 and 507 models had continued in production. Pneumatic tyres suitable for two-axle double-deckers had been developed and examples began to appear on AEC chassis early in 1927. A covered-top 409, the first NS on pneumatics, was supplied to the fleet of Greyhound Motors Ltd, then an enterprising independent operator based in Bristol. The first batch of 10 507 models for Birmingham Corporation also introduced pneumatics and that operator added more until a fleet of 128 was built up when the last entered service early in 1929. Thus this fleet accounted for over half the total of 240 of the 507 model built. Some of the remainder were goods, and the 506 almost entirely so — the latter continued to be delivered as late as 1932, by which date the total reached 530.

Realisation of a demand for the pneumatic-tyred NS led to it being put into production as model 422 later in 1927. It also incorporated a detachable-head version of the 4-type engine, type A128, basically similar to the A127 offered in later 416A models. The first 70 constituted a repeat order for Argentina, but 56 went to the LGOC, by then permitted to use 7ft 6in-wide buses, plus 29 for various municipal and company fleets in Britain supplied up to 1929.

At the November 1927 Show, in addition to an 802 in Birmingham colours, the first examples of the promised new single-deckers appeared: types 423 (forward-control) and 424 (bonneted). These were developed by Daimler at Coventry and showed the influence of Pomeroy in the widespread use of aluminium alloy and the adoption of a

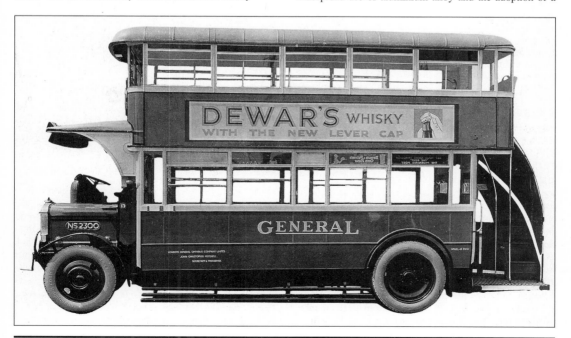

Top:
The 417 was the bonneted equivalent of the 416, and tended to be favoured by coach operators. With suitable bodywork, such vehicles had looks not too far removed from those of a large high-grade touring car of the day. This example with Hall Lewis body of 1928 for A. Timpson & Sons Ltd of Catford had a folding hood although at the rear a section of fixed roof supported a luggage carrier. *AEC/Author's collection*

Above:
The great hopes for ADC after a difficult first year were the new Daimler-designed 423 and 424 models introduced at the November 1927 Show. The Daimler CV25 six-cylinder sleeve-valve engine was supposed to be cured of its earlier problems, and with a neat appearance the model must have seemed very promising. Seen here is No 432002, built in time to act as a demonstrator during the show and bodied by United Automobile Services Ltd for the Crosville Motor Co Ltd, the latter of growing size and importance as well as a major Leyland user. *AEC/Author's collection*

radiator very like that of Daimler cars of the day, though lacking the characteristic fluted top. The CV25 engine was used and on paper the models must have seemed appealing, attracting quite substantial orders. However, the unreliability problems had still not been overcome. It was decided to build limited numbers at Coventry pending their resolution. In the event, many orders were cancelled and

only 73 of the 423 and 56 of the 424 were built, far fewer than hoped.

To fill the gap, a facelift of the 416 and 417 was carried out by fitting the style of radiator and bonnet of the 423 and 424 to otherwise unaltered chassis, the resulting models being given the type numbers 426 (of which 226 were built) and 427 (52 built). Type 425 was another 'United special' with the new radiator and the 4-type engine but having a longer wheelbase — of these 125 were built.

From about the beginning of 1928, the relationship between AEC and Daimler had become increasingly difficult, and a gradual distancing of the two firms became evident. Partly this stemmed from problems of divided ownership and management, especially when the two parent companies had businesses so divergent in character. Yet in practical terms the problems of the Daimler engines seriously damaged the prospects of success. The Daimler Co itself made a loss in 1927 and 1928, the recession of that period not helping sales of expensive cars.

By July 1928, the divorce was agreed and AEC and Daimler once again went their separate ways. Existing models were again referred to as AEC — the 422, 426, 427, 506 and 507 continuing to be available as such. Daimler based a new and fairly successful model called the CF6 on the chassis design of the 423 and 424 but using the larger CV35 engine, but AEC took a more radical path.

Above:
The problems with later models threw ADC back to the 416A with four-cylinder side-valve engine as the main single-deck model which it could sell with confidence. It is significant that in the spring of 1928 the LGOC, with experience of the CV25 sleeve-valve engine in earlier 419-model coaches, took delivery of a fleet of 416A coaches for private hire and touring. Ten had 28-seat bodies of the style shown, built by LGOC.
AEC/Ian Allan Library

Below:
Among the last steps taken by ADC in its brief and faltering career was the face-lift of the 416 model with the Daimler-style radiator from the 423, the result being designated 426. This example, photographed on the test hill at Southall, was for Samuelson's Saloon Coaches Ltd and carried a route board for a London-Liverpool service. The 426's polished aluminium covers completely encasing the dumb-irons rather than merely covering the top as on the 423 provided an identification point.
AEC/Author's collection

5. Rackham's Revolution

Just as the ADC era was ending, AEC received an application from George John Rackham for the position of Chief Engineer, a post that had remained vacant since Iden's departure in 1916, although Charles Edwards remained as Chief Designer.

G. J. Rackham (John only to those who knew him well) had joined Vanguard as a draughtsman in 1906, leaving to become Chief Draughtsman with LGOC the following year at the age of 22 and being one of the design team responsible for the X and B buses. He transferred to the newly formed AEC as Chief Draughtsman in 1912 but left

in 1916, and by 1917 was one of a War Office team involved in tank design, where he worked with George A. Green, another ex-LGOC man who had gone to manage the Fifth Avenue Coach Co in New York in 1912. In 1922, Green invited him to become Chief Engineer of the Yellow Coach Manufacturing Co Ltd in Chicago. There he was responsible for a series of bus designs widely used in the USA. It is significant that a 1927 Yellow single-decker had been chosen by Lord Ashfield (whose early career had also blossomed in the United States) for use as a personal 'parlour coach'.

Meanwhile Rackham had returned to England to become Chief Engineer of Leyland Motors Ltd in 1926, setting about the design of the trend-setting Leyland Titan TD1 double-decker. This dominated the November 1927 Show, underlining the

Left:
Rackham's first task on arrival at Southall in the summer of 1928 was to supervise the design of the new 6-type overhead-camshaft six-cylinder petrol engine. As with most things for which he was responsible, it was of elegant design, and proved a reliable, smooth-running and lively power unit, the key to a whole range of highly successful chassis types. This early example is of the original A130 type with sump and exposed flywheel to suit the Reliance chassis.
AEC/Author's collection

failure of ADC's 802 by its immediate and wide-ranging sales success — notable among early customers was Glasgow Corporation, with an initial order for 15 and then one for 100 in August 1928.

His return to AEC was confirmed on 3 July 1928, with an allegedly very high salary and considerable freedom of action. Amazingly, by 29 September the first example of a new engine he designed was on test. Many stories of doubtful authenticity have been told about Rackham, always a controversial figure, but I was told by eye-witnesses in the drawing office that when a query arose, his assistant George Robinson, who came to Southall from Leyland with him, would be dispatched to his office to fetch a Leyland blueprint and the designer would be instructed to 'make it like that'. So the resulting 6-type six-cylinder engine, with its overhead-

camshaft layout, had a strong visual resemblance to the Leyland T-type engine, yet it was by no means a straight copy. The cylinder dimensions of the original basic A130 engine were smaller, giving a swept volume of 6.1 litres instead of the T-type's 6.8 litres, yet the 95bhp output was almost the same, using slightly higher revs. Smooth, quiet power, reliability and durability were characteristics of both units.

With this engine, Rackham had the first key element of a new range of models. Yet he was faced with a considerable stock of existing chassis and parts rapidly becoming unsaleable. By fitting the new 6-type engine into a slightly modified 426 chassis, an effective interim model resulted, given the name Reliance with model number 660. A distinctive new feature of the production chassis was the appearance of the AEC bull's-eye motif on a new triangular radiator badge, mounted so that the point

Above:
A clearer indication of the direction AEC's design policy was taking was given by the new Regent model. The first supplied to an operator was the second chassis, No 661002, which became the National Omnibus & Transport Co Ltd's No 2902, registered VW 9565 and delivered to NOTC's Colchester branch on 12 April 1929. The body, built by Short Bros to an AEC design used for many of the earliest Regents, had echoes of Leyland's style as built for the TD1 model, notably in its profile. *AEC/Author's collection*

Left:
The LGOC's introduction to the new-generation AEC models was the arrival of the first of the Renown six-wheelers, chassis number 663001, which became fleet number LT1. Seen here when new and in a short-lived livery of red with cream upperworks, it entered service in August 1929. The Chiswick-built 54-seat body retained some LS-like details but established the profile to be standard for LGOC double-deckers built until the end of 1931 — rather conservative yet blending well with the outline of the new AEC radiator. *AEC/Ian Allan Library*

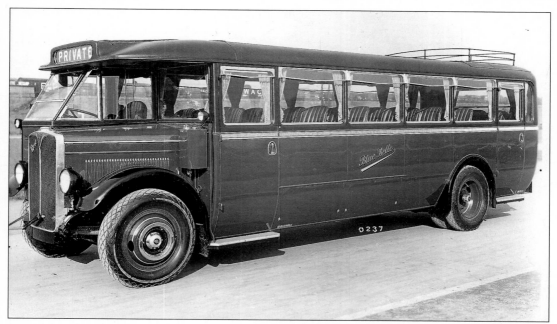

Above:
The Regal single-decker, model 662, also introduced in 1929, shared most of its design features with the Regent. Blue Belle Motors Ltd of London SW2 took delivery of a batch with bodywork by London Lorries early in 1930, including the example here. Six were taken over in 1932 by Green Line Coaches Ltd, passing to London Transport.
AEC/Author's collection

Below:
By the time the new models were put into production, the outline of the radiator grille had been subtly altered to blend better with the triangle badge. This Newcastle Corporation Regent with body by Hall Lewis was delivered in January 1930, and was later to be one of the buses which first aroused the author's interest in the make, over 60 years ago. It is seen in the Haymarket in that city, in company with United ADC 425 and 415 single-deckers. *AEC/Author's collection*

The Regent was chosen by the LGOC to replace the K-type buses, and bulk deliveries of the resulting ST-class with the style of 49-seat body basically as shown took place during much of 1930 and 1931, occupying most of the fleet numbers up to ST836. They had enclosed stairs but the Metropolitan Police was still unhappy about the provision of windscreens and hence most, like ST513, bodied at Chiswick and new in September 1930, were delivered with open cab as shown. Officialdom relented the following spring and windscreens were then fitted. *Ian Allan Library*

Below left:
The long-wheelbase version of the Renown six-wheeler was given the type number 664 and the largest purchaser was the LGOC, placing 199 in service

with Chiswick-built 35-seat single-deck bodywork on suburban services in 1931. Two almost identical buses were built in 1932 for London General Country Services but later joined the others in London Transport's central-area fleet — LT1427 is seen at Chislehurst in postwar days. *F. G. Reynolds*

Above right:
The original Mercury was the lightest model in the 6-type goods range introduced in autumn 1929. At first it was offered in bonneted form only as type 640, rated at 3½-ton payload capacity and having a four-cylinder petrol engine of similar overhead-camshaft design to the six-cylinder version. At first, it did not have front wheel brakes as standard. It is possible to

read the chassis number 640124 stamped on the nearside dumb-iron in the original of this official view. *AEC/Ian Allan Library*

Below:
This Mercury first registered early in 1931 and operated by A. A. Harvey of Aldershot is seen in use during World War 2 — no doubt there was plenty of work for it in that military town. By 1942 it had covered 300,000 miles and had 'never seen the end of a tow-rope', yet the engine did not receive a major overhaul until February 1941. The general appearance and many of the visible chassis details had clear affinities to the passenger range. *AEC/Ian Allan Library*

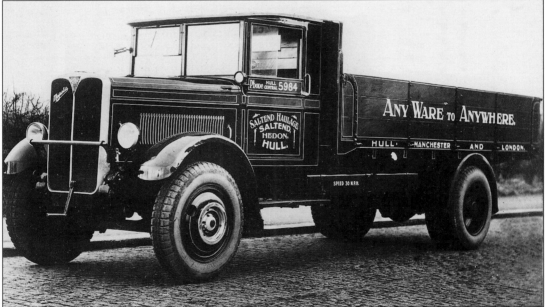

Top:
The Monarch 641 was a forward-control equivalent of the Mercury, but rated for a 4-ton load. Early examples usually had a square-cut style of cab as shown here, and the positioning of the headlamps to allow them to serve also as sidelamps gave an effect unusual at that date. The Danish Bacon Co Ltd, based in Hull, soon placed an order for eight, this example with van body entering service early in 1930.
AEC/Ian Allan Library

Above:
The appearance of the Majestic lived up to its name, noticeably taller as well as larger than the Mercury. The nominal load rating was 6 tons but the design allowed for trailer haulage, and the six-cylinder petrol engine was opened up in bore size to give a 7.4-litre capacity. This example dates from 1930. *Ian Allan Library*

Above:
The heaviest rated of the goods range introduced in late 1929 was the Mammoth, model 667, of forward-control layout. By the latter part of 1931, when this example for Yeoman of Canterbury was built, the standard cab style incorporated a sloping windscreen and what was to be the typical appearance of an AEC lorry for the next few years was established. The 666 and 667 had fully floating rear axles with large hubs, unlike other AEC models of the period. *Ian Allan Library*

Below:
The Ranger, model 665, was a bonneted equivalent of the Regal. This 1931 example with Harrington 26-seat body was supplied to Grey Cars, originally a Torquay-based subsidiary of A. Timpson & Son Ltd of London, but taken over in 1933 by Devon General, though continuing to be operated as a separate touring coach fleet. *AEC/Ian Allan Library*

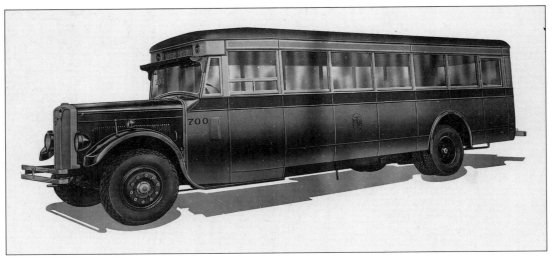

Above:
The left-hand-drive version of the Ranger was type 670, this example entering service in Montreal. *AEC/Author's collection*

Below:
The use of low-loading passenger-type chassis for goods applications aroused considerable interest for a time, although only limited numbers were built. The first such case in the 6-type AEC range was on an early Regent chassis, No 661037, delivered to the Anglo-American Oil Co Ltd in December 1929. *AEC/Author's collection*

projected downwards over the core. I was told by Rackham that Lord Ashfield had seen something similar on a visit to Germany. The Adler car of the time fits the description — an illustration of how detailed Ashfield's interest in such matters could be.

The Reliance was introduced at the end of 1928 and was AEC's main passenger model for most of 1929, though the last of the total of 484 built were not sold until 1932, some especially at the beginning and end of production being rebuilt from stock 426 or 416 chassis. Meanwhile, work was going ahead on an entirely new range of models worthy of the new engine.

The first was a new double-decker, model 661, given perhaps the most famous of all AEC model names, Regent, of which the prototype chassis was at the bodybuilders by February 1929. By that summer a dozen pre-production examples had been built. There were many resemblances in the chassis design to the Titan TD1 although the front-end layout was tidier and more compact, setting a standard for appearance which was widely copied over the next few years. The further development of the 'blue triangle' radiator produced the distinctive style thereafter most associated with AEC.

Top:
The original Mandator was designed specifically as a low-loading goods model, having the lower build of the passenger chassis but using the heavy-duty double-reduction goods rear axle. A dozen of the forward-control version, type 669, were built, this one for an operator based in Reigate having a Park Royal insulated van body and dating from early 1932.
Author's collection

Above:
Seen here is an example of the bonneted Mandator, model 672, of which seven were built in 1931-2, in this case with tanker body by Butterfield of Shipley in the livery of the Texaco concern, dating from early 1932. The design was modelled quite faithfully in a Dinky Toy of the later 1930s. Similar bodywork was also built on some Ranger chassis. *AEC/Author's collection*

In mechanical design, the use of a gearbox directly attached to the engine, a rear axle with offset differential casing and semi-floating axle shafts were all TD1 and indeed Yellow features. The layout allowed a gangway height as low as that of the NS without the complexity of the latter's rear axle. The semi-floating construction of the axle might be criticised as a 'cheap Americanism' and indeed in the early 1930s both Leyland and AEC reverted to fully floating axles after reports of failures, yet plenty of the earlier types gave little trouble over long lives.

In due course, legal action by Leyland over the similarity of design is said to have been planned but nothing significant happened. The range as announced publicly in the autumn of 1929 also included the Regal, model 662, which was a single-decker of similar design to the Regent, and a pair of three-axle models, types 663 and 664, of short and long wheelbase respectively, for which the name Renown was revived. Rackham was, correctly, convinced that the future lay with two-axle buses, yet the Renown was by far the most successful three-axle bus of the time.

Engine type numbers became quite complex during this period, partly because more variations were being covered — for example, the first 12 Regents had type A131, but production variations of basically the same engine had type numbers A136, A137 and A138 according to dynamo size, while A140 had a Scintilla magneto, much favoured by LGOC.

Above:
AEC's publicity department was always on the look-out for striking pictures and this one of Western National No 2963, a 1930 Regal with Strachans 32-seat body, well laden with holiday-makers and their luggage, ascending Porlock Hill in Somerset appeared in several advertisements.
AEC/Ian Allan Library

At first, however, the attitude to AEC on the part of the LGOC remained guarded. It is noteworthy that while the new models were still in the prototype stage approval was given for LGOC to design and build prototype buses of its own design at Chiswick, something which Ashfield could surely have scotched if so minded. Four LGOC CC-type six-wheel double-deckers and three CB two-axle single-deckers were built in 1930-1 but the AEC models had meanwhile proved entirely successful.

Only one of the initial 12 Regents went to LGOC and was diverted to East Surrey, so the first of the new-generation AECs with a body by LGOC to its requirements was on the initial Renown 663-type six-wheeled chassis, which was given the fleet number LT1 and entered service in August 1929. This had an open-staircase double-deck body, as did 149 more completed in 1930. The first Regent for LGOC's own fleet was numbered ST1 and was licensed in October, this time with enclosed-stair body.

By that date the replacement of the K and S-types was about to begin, so the ST, mostly seating 49 as built, and the LT, seating 60 or 56 (the latter for those built with enclosed stairs in 1931), gave a striking advance in comfort and performance. The fleet numbers rose to ST836, completed by May 1931, and LT950, by the end of that year — in both cases there were small numbers of

non-standard examples within those ranges, some important in their implications. In 1932 came a further 273 LT-class Renown double-deckers with 60 seats and enclosed stairs.

Similarly, the Regal single-decker was given the class letter T by LGOC, with an initial 50 buses at the end of 1929. In addition, this model with more luxurious bodywork was adopted by Green Line Coaches Ltd, a new LGOC associate establishing what would nowadays be called commuter coach services, which, with other batches, took the fleet numbers to T306 by early 1931. There were also 200 of the long-wheelbase Renown 664 chassis, all but one with single-deck bodies for LGOC suburban services.

To these buses for LGOC and associates were added numerous orders from provincial operators of all types; for the first time, AEC was building large numbers of basically similar passenger chassis for service in London and elsewhere. By mid-1933, about 5,000 of the 6-type passenger models had been built — the renewal of LGOC's fleet accounted for roundly half of this. In addition to some very important new options described later, various design changes were made during the early years of these models, including improvements to items such as brakes and steering, often inspired by LGOC experience. One of the great strengths of AEC was the benefit of the immense practical knowledge of running the world's largest bus fleet, carrying large passenger loads in what was often heavy traffic even then.

A new 6-type goods model range with similar design characteristics to the passenger types was also added in time for the 1929 Show. There were two pairs of types:

the Mercury 640 being a bonneted 3½-ton model, and the Monarch 641, a 4-ton forward control type, both with a four-cylinder 5.1-litre (112mm x 130mm) version of the 6-type engine, A139, and overhead worm rear axles. At the other end of the scale were the Majestic 666 bonneted 6-tonner and the Mammoth 667 forward-control 7/8-ton type. These had double-reduction bevel axles and a version of the six-cylinder engine with bore increased to 110mm, giving a 7.4-litre swept volume — they were intended to haul separate two-axle trailers. Sales were relatively modest; the best-selling type was the Mammoth, of which 384 were built by 1935.

The 7.4-litre engine also began to be offered on passenger models and then became standard, notably in type A145 as used on much of LGOC's LT class from 1931. An improved 'high-power head' version giving 120bhp — type A162 — became standard for most six-cylinder models from 1932.

AEC's design department kept up the torrent of new types. One of the more significant in 1931 was a 12-ton six-wheeler, model 668, which was given what at first must have seemed a rather lame title, Mammoth Major, even though it became one of AEC's most famous types. In all, 365 were built up to 1939, though the 668 was superseded for general home-market use after 1935.

Other new types were largely derived from existing units, such as the Ranger, a bonneted version of the Regal, model 665 or 670, the latter with left-hand steering; the Regal 4, model 642, which had the four-cylinder engine, as did the Marshal 644 military six-wheeler, and the original Matador 645, a forward-control 5-ton model. The first Mandators were low-loading goods models

(669 being forward-control and the 672 normal-control). There were also new trolleybus chassis based on the main passenger models, 661T being the two-axle double-decker, for example; although demand was modest at first, it was to grow later in the 1930s.

Of deeper significance were the first AEC oil (diesel) engines. A unit of this type had been the subject of experimental running in the 802-type 104-seat works bus as early as 1928, this work being supervised by Charles Edwards, though he left the company in 1929. The previous year Cedric B. Dicksee joined AEC as an engine designer and in October 1930, AEC's first production engine, type A155, was announced. It was of 8.1-litre capacity, with 110mm bore and 142mm stroke, and the claimed output was 95bhp, matching the early 6-type petrol engine but it was about $4\frac{1}{2}$in longer than that unit so buses fitted with it had the radiator thrust forward by this amount (this becoming a characteristic of many oil-engined AECs until early 1935 and sometimes later). Three entered service in LGOC ST buses by the end of the year, but the nine in LT-type Renown double-deckers from March 1931 set a pattern, that model not being subject to

such tight limitations on weight and length, so most of LGOC's considerable work on oil engines involved this class. Examples of the A155 were supplied to quite a number of other operators early in 1931 but soon an epidemic of thrown conn-rods, smashed crankcases and other failures was being experienced, partly because these early engines were ungoverned and could run to high speeds, creating unforeseen stresses.

The aid of the Ricardo engine development consultancy was sought and the first application of this concern's Comet combustion system was the resulting AEC oil engine, with cylinder bore increased to 115mm and 8.8-litre swept volume, announced in September 1931. In production in A165 form, this was to be AEC's main engine of this type until early 1935, giving up to 130bhp and being reliable if not always easy to start from cold. Some 62 of the LT-class buses built in 1932 were so fitted from new in addition to earlier conversions and the foundation for later progress was laid.

The traditional clutch and sliding-mesh gearbox was far from satisfactory for urban bus work, requiring a fair amount of skill in use and frequent renewals. Walter Gordon Wilson, whom Rackham met when on tank work, had developed a preselective epicyclic gearbox eliminating the need for skill in timing gear changes and Daimler had combined this with a fluid coupling (which it christened 'fluid flywheel') giving smooth starting from

Above:
In October 1930, AEC was the first British commercial vehicle maker to offer an oil (diesel) engine as a production option. It required a somewhat awkward-looking installation in passenger models, with the radiator set forward and slightly raised, as seen on this Regent with Short Bros body for Stockton Corporation, one of several sent out to operators early in 1931. The 8.1-litre Acro-head A155 engine proved troublesome but was the basis for a much improved design later that year. *AEC/Author's collection*

Above right:
Thanks to an initiative by Lord Ashfield, AEC was allowed to use the combination of fluid flywheel and Wilson preselective epicyclic gearbox developed by Daimler. An early installation was in one of the first 16ft 3in wheelbase AEC Regent chassis, supplied to E. Brickwood Ltd of London W10 trading as Red Line. It was fitted with a 1930 Birch Bros body removed from a Daimler CF6 and is seen here at AEC's works before entering service in March 1932. After being taken over by LPTB in December 1933, it became STL558. *AEC/Ian Allan Library*

Right:
Much of the AEC and LGOC work on oil engines in 1931-2 related to the latter's LT-class Renown double-deckers. Some of the later batches with what became known as the 'Bluebird' 60-seat type of body had the A165 8.8-litre Ricardo Comet-head type of engine from new. LT1380, dating from September 1932, was one of 30 which combined it with the crash gearbox — it is seen in postwar days and survived until 1949. *B. V. Franey*

rest, offering it on its own cars and buses from late 1930.

Lord Ashfield was impressed and three Daimler CH6 buses so fitted entered service with LGOC in February 1931. It was greatly to Ashfield's credit that he saw the potential of their success almost immediately. Moreover, despite the break-up of ADC only three years earlier, the relationship between him and Daimler was such that he was able to persuade the latter to supply AEC with fluid flywheels and Wilson gearboxes for fitting into its buses. This applied not only for LGOC (74 were in use in LT-class buses by the end of 1932) but for sale in AEC chassis generally, a type of agreement denied to those of Daimler's car competitors who took up the Wilson gearbox, who had to manage without the fluid flywheel. The fluid transmission option was available on AECs from 1932 and was taken up by numbers of operators, largely municipalities although also some coach users — indeed more such sets were supplied to AEC than used in Daimler's own buses up to 1934, when AEC began making its own units of this type.

As if all this was not enough, in 1932 there appeared Rackham's most adventurous bus design, the side-engined AEC Q. Again, there was American influence, for Fageol had introduced a model called the Twin-Coach in 1925, the name deriving from its use of two engines, one mounted on each side between the axles. The AEC version had one engine, mounted behind the offside front wheel, and a key feature was the setting back of the rear axle to reduce the weight it carried. This permitted the use of single rear tyres and allowed the differential to be well over to the offside, giving an almost straight transmission line. The prototype of the single-decker, model 762, with suitably adapted 7.4-litre petrol engine and crash gearbox, entered experimental service with the LGOC as Q1 on 5 September 1932 on route 11, one of the capital's busiest, run by LT-class double-deckers. It proved much slower at stops — hardly surprising in view of its single narrow doorway just behind the front axle — and was soon moved to other duties.

Rackham conceived the Q more especially as a double-decker, model 761, and its front-end layout of 65 years ago was remarkably close to what much later became normal practice, even though it took about half that time to become established. In this case, the front axle was set back, as on the Twin-Coach as well as some early trolleybuses, and hence the entrance platform was alongside the driver, with the staircase running up over the front offside wheel in the manner now commonplace. At the time, the Q seemed almost weird, with no radiator at the front, and Rackham's ideas on appearance, as encapsulated in Q body designs registered by AEC, were also to prove visually influential.

This first Q double-decker had fluid transmission, adopted as standard for all later Qs. It visited Chiswick later that same month, though with no immediate reaction. It was a demonstrator, sent to Birmingham Corporation early in 1933, and nine more double-deckers were put in hand to be sent out to potential customers.

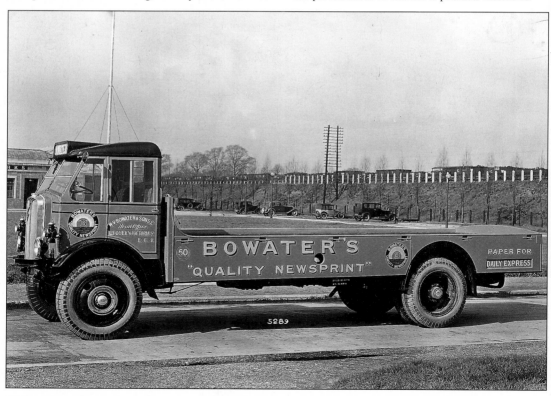

Left:
AEC lorries delivered the paper for many of the national daily newspapers over a long period; Bowater's placed this stylish oil-engined Mammoth in service early in 1933. Some operators were still unconvinced of the reliability of electric lighting and the use of railway-style oil lamps as side lights is noteworthy. *AEC/Author's collection*

Above:
The AEC Q was a remarkably advanced concept, its side engine position allowing a front-end layout very like that usual on modern buses. This picture of the first double-deck example, No 761001, on demonstration duty in Birmingham in the early summer of 1933 could almost be mistaken for a relatively modern scene were it not for the styles of clothing of those boarding. The Metro-Cammell body was built to an AEC-registered design. *AEC/Author's collection*

Above:
The 'Land Cruiser' was the name given to this remarkable vehicle, completed in June 1933 for the personal use of Capt Macmullen, seen (left), with E. Harrington of Thos. Harrington Ltd, responsible for the bodywork. It combined contemporary coach and cabin cruiser ideas, with art deco touches. There was a lounge, galley and steward's sleeping compartment downstairs, with double and single bedrooms above. It was based on a Regal chassis — presumably the 17ft 6in wheelbase was preferred — and had the standard 120bhp petrol engine of the day. In wartime, it was pressed into use as workers' transport by A. & C. Wickman, machine tool makers. *Ian Allan Library*

Below:
The Regal 4, model 642, with four-cylinder engine, was sold only in modest numbers. This demonstrator is thought to have been 642010, initially ordered at the end of 1931 but later updated with fully floating rear axle, identifiable by its larger hub, and, early in 1933, fitted with an A166 oil engine, bodied by Park Royal and registered at that date as AMD 47. It was later sold to Newbury & District. The Regal 4 looked much the same as a standard Regal, though the four-cylinder oil engine had a slightly higher-mounted oil filler and a prominent broad sump, just catching the light in this view. *Author's collection*

6. Variety in the Later 1930s

AEC was floated as a separate business from 1 July 1933 as a consequence of the formation of the London Passenger Transport Board, the latter taking over the main part of the Underground group as the nucleus of a unified transport system for London and retaining much of LGOC practice in regard to buses. In one sense, AEC was thereby launched into quite a hostile world, for the depression of the early 1930s was about at its worst — combined bus sales of all makes in Britain in 1933 were only a third of what they had been in 1930. Even so, the reborn AEC again had a silver spoon in its mouth: an agreement to supply not less than 90% of LPTB's motorbus chassis in the period up to 1944.

The first decision relating to bus policy of the LPTB was to standardise on oil engines for future purchases — at about the same time AEC adopted the O prefix on model and chassis numbers to signify oil-engined models. However, the LGOC had decided to revert to two-axle Regent chassis for its largest double-deckers, using a longer-wheelbase version to take advantage of a slight increase in permitted length; these it classified the STL-type. They entered service from the beginning of 1933, initially with bodies seating 60, though from later in the

year reduced to 56. This design would not accept the A165 8.8-litre oil engine without loss of seating capacity, so initially 339 such engines were purchased to convert petrol LT-class buses, their petrol engines going into new STLs.

A four-cylinder oil engine had been added to AEC's range earlier in 1933 largely for use in goods models, this being built in two forms, A166 and A168, having bore sizes of 108mm or 120mm respectively and 146mm stroke, giving swept volumes of 5.35 or 6.6 litres. A more compact six-cylinder engine was also introduced, initially for the Q side-engined passenger models, the intention being that it would be of 7.7-litre size. The bore and stroke were to be 106mm and 146mm, but it seems that, by mistake and too

Below:
The newly formed London Transport decided to standardise on oil engines for future buses and on the STL-class 56-seat 16ft 3in-wheelbase Regent double-decker. The two aims were not at first compatible and a process of fitting new A165 8.8-litre oil engines to existing LT-class buses and transferring their 110mm-bore 7.4-litre petrol engines to the new buses was adopted. Seen here when new in May 1934 is STL433, one of 100 with AEC preselective gearboxes. *LT/Ian Allan Library*

Above left:
The 8.8-litre oil-engined Regent made a significant breakthrough with Rhondda Tramways Ltd, being chosen for a tram-replacement batch of 30 buses delivered in the winter of 1933-4 after comparative tests involving a Bristol G, a Dennis Lance and a Leyland Titan. This was the first major order for oil-engined AEC buses from a BET-controlled company. In this case a 52-seat capacity was considered acceptable — the metal-framed body was by Weymann. *AEC/Author's collection*

Left:
The original Matador, model 645, was a 5-ton model marrying a four-cylinder engine with the heavy-duty axles of the early six-cylinder goods models. This example dating from late 1933 was noteworthy in being oil-engined, using the A168 6.6-litre four-cylinder unit introduced earlier that year, the designation then becoming O645. *Ian Allan Library*

Above:
Another instance of AEC being associated with futuristic transport ideas was the first of the diesel railcars built for the Great Western Railway in 1933. Strictly speaking, the 'chassis' was made by Hardy Motors Ltd, though that concern was by then based at Southall, and the type number fitted into the AEC series as O852, the engine being an 8.8-litre unit modified to suit the installation. It is seen just after completion of the body, built by Park Royal. Some of the purity of line of this original was lost in later versions as the need for conventional buffer and coupling gear was accepted. *Author's collection*

late to rectify before prototypes were built, the actual bore was 105mm and hence the capacity became 7.58 litres and remained thus in production.

Thus was born one of AEC's most famous engine series, always known as the 'seven seven' despite the discrepancy. The Q version was type A170, introduced in mid-1933. It was followed by the A171 for front-engined models, first tried in 11 STL buses early in 1934 and becoming standard at the end of that year from STL 609. It was adopted as the standard oil engine across AEC's six-cylinder range in place of the 8.8 from spring 1935. Another change introduced in 1934 was AEC manufacture of the optional preselective gearbox, no longer purchased from Daimler. The LPTB put nearly 1,900 STL buses with the A171 engine and AEC-built Wilson gearboxes into service up to mid-1938.

Sales of AEC oil engines for the conversion of existing vehicles or for use by other chassis makers grew at around this time, the latter including some of the own-make vehicles of the Midland Red concern as well as modest numbers of Bristol and Daimler buses, the latter for the Coventry municipal fleet. In addition, use for marine or industrial applications gradually grew into a sizeable business.

Much was made of the Q at the 1933 Commercial Motor Show, but sales were poor, especially of the double-decker. The LPTB took four in 1934 but remained committed to the STL for its bulk orders, and no other operator had more than two. The single-decker did a little better, attracting most of its modest sales from independent

coach operators until the LPTB came to the rescue with successive orders for 100 country buses, 80 central-area buses and 50 Green Line coaches in 1935-7, all being oil-engined, as was becoming usual in all major fleets. In the event, some changed function and with an extra couple of buses and a unique six-wheel Q double-deck coach, model O763, the LPTB fleet of the type ran up to Q238.

AEC's total sales of two-axle Q double-deckers amounted to a mere 23, plus five of a 761T trolleybus version, and there were 316 single-deckers — not quite a disaster but far short of what had been hoped, not least by Rackham himself. The model was quietly dropped in 1937.

Another futuristic-seeming venture of 1933 was the streamlined railcar, most unusually also exhibited at the Commercial Motor Show and catching the public imagination. It was publicised as an AEC product, though actually made by Hardy Motors Ltd, which had been formed in 1931 to take over production at AEC's works of cross-country vehicles which had been basically of FWD design and hitherto made in Slough (using AEC engines from 1929), as well as taking up Hardy's interest in rail applications. The railcar was for the Great Western

Above:
The Regal was strongly favoured by several major London independent coach operators. A. Timpson & Sons Ltd of Catford was running 95 AEC coaches in a total fleet of 106 in 1935. The firm specialised in large company outings and this scene taking place outside the premises of CAV-Bosch Ltd in Acton dates from 1938, though the leading coach, with Harrington body, was new in 1933 and most of the others visible date from 1930. *Ian Allan Library*

Below:
Revised legislation fostered a new Mark II range of goods models, lighter than their predecessors, introduced in April 1935. The Monarch II, type O344, built to suit the 12-ton gross weight limit, continued to have a four-cylinder engine but now had a worm-drive rear axle as standard. It became the most popular AEC goods model of the later 1930s. This example dating from early 1936 was supplied to A. Hughes of Hawarden near Chester but the HG index mark suggests it may have been registered by Tillotson of Burnley, a major AEC distributor. *AEC/Ian Allan Library*

Top:
The 7.7-litre engine in A171 form was adopted as standard for the six-cylinder range from early 1935, having the virtue of being directly interchangeable with the petrol unit and not requiring the projecting radiator. City of Oxford Motor Services Ltd, which standardised on AEC buses from 1930 to 1967 with very few exceptions, had favoured petrol engines until adopting the 7.7 from 1935. Seen here is one of 11 Regents with Weymann metal-framed lowbridge bodies delivered in early 1936. *Ian Allan Library*

Above:
The four-cylinder Mercury, latterly rated at 10 tons gross, continued in production until 1937. The forward-control 641 van in Craven A cigarette livery in this dockside scene dated from late 1936. The Monarch name previously used for the 641 was now reserved for 12-ton-gross four-cylinder models. *Ian Allan Library*

Top:
What generally became known as the standard STL, with 7.7-litre A171 engine, preselective gearbox and the characteristic style of body having a gently curved profile, first appeared in November 1934. Nearly 1,900 such buses, including some specialised variants and mostly with Chiswick-built bodies, were on London's streets by the time this photograph at Broad Street was taken in August 1938. Three of them, led by STL888 dating from December 1935, are evident in the line-up of six buses, the others being an ST and two LTs. *LT Museum*

Above:
The Mammoth Major eight-wheeler as redesigned in Mark II form from 1935 became model O386. It now had the 7.7-litre engine as standard — vehicles with suitably light bodies such as these two built for Liverpool Cartage Co Ltd late in 1935 and weighing 6 tons 12cwt unladen would have been able to carry 15 tons while keeping within the 22-ton gross weight limit applicable at that time. The cabs and bodies were by Park Royal. *Author's collection*

Railway and used an 8.8-litre oil engine driving through a preselective gearbox, becoming the first of 38 railcars for the GWR built up to 1940.

The initials FWD signified Four Wheel Drive (4x4), and originally came from the pioneer American firm of that name. Hardy models inherited some of their features and, although built only in small numbers, provided the basis for later AEC expansion in this field, as described in the next chapter.

Of wider significance was the eight-wheeled version of the Mammoth Major, model 680, introduced early in 1934. Sentinel had built its DG8 steam lorry of this layout in 1929, but AEC pioneered the rigid eight-wheeler as a motor vehicle, although the concept was very soon taken up by others. Only 34 of the 680 model were built, finishing in 1935, but this was because new regulations put greater emphasis on unladen weight and AEC introduced a new Mark II goods range of lighter construction.

A revised model numbering system related to basic specification was brought in for the Mark II goods models, the first digit signifying bonneted (2) or forward-control (3), the second the number of wheels and the third the number of cylinders. Hence the Monarch was now O244 or O344, the Matador O246 or O346 and the Mammoth Major O366 or O386. The Mercury was not included, remaining as O640 if bonneted and O641 if forward-control — by that date, bonneted AEC models were becoming quite rare in Britain. The 'O' prefix was omitted when petrol engines were fitted, steadily becoming less common. Some 720 of the Monarch O344 or 344 types were built but the next most numerous type in the Mark II goods range was the Mammoth Major eight-wheeler, with 521 built up to early wartime.

Among passenger types, demand for the orthodox

Above:
Another new line of development was the introduction of a lighter single-decker, christened the Regal Mark II, model O862. It had a new six-cylinder oil engine of nominal 6.6-litre size, but the chassis weight saving was only 6cwt and sales proved limited. This was the first one, with Weymann 34-seat body, exhibited at the Commercial Show in November 1935. Rhondda Transport Co Ltd took a further eight a few months later. The radiator style, with chromium-plated shell, was unique to this model. *AEC/Author's collection*

Regent and Regal dipped somewhat in the recession of 1933-4, but even so remained far above that for the Q, and then expanded strongly in the later 1930s, aided by the big LPTB orders. In the peak prewar year for the Regent, 1937, over 1,100 were delivered, of which about 700 were London STL buses. The demand for six-wheel motorbuses dropped, so sales of Renown models were small after 1932.

On the other hand, some 831 of the corresponding 664T trolleybus were built between 1935 and 1942, strongly outnumbering the two-axle 661T double-decker which was runner-up among AEC trolleybuses, with 380 in the 1931-41 period. There had been a big upsurge in demand for trolleybuses, often six-wheelers, in that period, mainly for tram replacement. Three-quarters of the 664T models were for the LPTB, beginning in 1935, though in fact Leyland supplied a slightly greater number.

The Q was not quite the only passenger model to have modest sales. The four-cylinder Regal 4 sold rather slowly, totalling 177 in the period up to 1937. A lighter model introduced in 1935 was the Regal Mark II, model O862, with a new six-cylinder oil engine, the A172, of 105mm x 130mm cylinder dimensions and 6.75-litre swept volume, though known as the 6.6-litre in line with the usual AEC

pattern. It had what were known as 'wet' cylinder liners, in direct contact with the cooling water, a system that proved prone to gasket trouble. A petrol version of this engine, type A174, was added as an option, but combined sales of the O862 and 862 only reached 104 by 1939.

AEC had placed strong faith in the Ricardo Comet indirect injection system for its oil engines but was conscious of operators' reports of better fuel economy from direct-injection engines, notably Gardner (a few of which had been fitted from new in AEC buses and lorries, though this was not publicised at the time) and Leyland. The first production AEC direct-injection engine was based on the '7.7' and was offered as an option, again without publicity, from 1936, designated A173. Early engines had quite a shallow combustion chamber in the piston crown but from about mid-1937 what was called the straight-sided toroidal cavity was adopted, with good economy and prompt starting in any weather among its merits. From then, it became increasingly popular, though AEC did not announce its availability as an economy option until July 1938. In practice, it was already the most popular choice — 132 new and 286 former petrol London STL buses were so fitted in 1939, though these were unusual in having flexible engine mountings.

By contrast, a few operators continued to specify the A165 Comet-head 8.8-litre engine where more power was

Above:
The 'standard' Regal, model O662, continued to be more widely favoured, and from 1937, some had early examples of the A173 direct-injection version of the 7.7-litre engine. The Bath Tramways Motor Co Ltd placed 20 such chassis with bodies by Eastern Coach Works in service in July 1937, two being seen here. This company, although having a hitherto mostly elderly AEC fleet, was by then a subsidiary of the Bristol Tramways & Carriage Co Ltd which generally built its own chassis, though also taking some new Regals as coaches in 1938. *AEC/Author's collection*

Right:
The need for a model with a mid-range weight capacity led to the introduction in 1937 of the Mammoth Minor, model O366L, with single-tyred rearmost axle. In all, 124 were built in the period up to 1941; this one with Lee Motors body, supplied to A. R. Holder & Sons of Deptford in the spring of 1938, was that firm's first vehicle with an oil engine and a tribute to its virtues appeared in the AEC Gazette August 1938 — with a 5-ton unladen weight, its operating costs were described as in the 8-ton class although it could carry 12-ton loads. It is seen here in wartime, well laden with timber. *AEC/Ian Allan Library*

required, but there was also interest, notably from London Transport, in a direct-injection version of this engine, put into production as type A180, the objectives here being more inclined to extended service life and refinement. The majority used a pot-shaped piston cavity, incorporated under licence from Leyland, which used a similar arrangement in its standard oil engine of the time — understandably, yet again there was no publicity.

The A180 engine was adopted both for 266 Green Line coaches on Regal chassis built in 1938, best known as the 10T10 type, and for a further large conversion programme for petrol-engined LT-class double-deckers, 550 being so fitted between 1938 and January 1940. There were also several orders for the A180 engine in Regent chassis,

mainly from municipal fleets, often with hilly routes, in 1938-40.

A major rethink had been set in train, encouraged by LPTB, favouring larger engines mainly on the basis of durability. In 1937 AEC had begun work on a completely redesigned 8.8-litre engine, more compact than the

Below:
Bonneted AEC models were rarely sold in Britain after the early 1930s, but this short-wheelbase Matador tractor was coupled to an Eagle 10-ton semi-trailer designed to carry cable drums for the Yorkshire Electric Power Co Ltd. The provision of a starting handle suggests that it was probably a petrol-engined 246. By then, the Matador was a six-cylinder type, so it was probably quite a gentlemanly machine to drive. *AEC/Ian Allan Library*

Above:
London Transport was by far the largest customer for the 664T trolleybus, itself AEC's most popular trolleybus model. The bodywork on the series of batches replacing London trams was built by various contractors, though always to LPTB's specified outline. No 597, seen here at AEC before delivery, was one of the 50 vehicles in the E1 class bodied by Brush dating from 1937. Like many London trolleybuses, most lasted over 20 years. *AEC/Author's collection*

Right:
The Matador O346 was designed with trailer haulage in mind. This example, operated by M. B. Down & Co Ltd, dating from early 1937, had done so from new, though seen here well laden with concrete pipes in wartime conditions in the summer of 1941. *AEC/Ian Allan Library*

A165/A180 and yet capable of being upgraded to have a larger capacity where needed — some prototypes were built and the engine was put into small-scale production as type A182. A few went into basically standard Regent chassis from 1938, others into Mammoth Major eight-wheelers and some into railcars.

There was also strong Chiswick involvement in a similarly new chassis incorporating one of these engines. The prototype emerged in 1938 for a brief spell of running with an old open-staircase body and then, in 1939, united with the Board's radically new design of body intended for it as RT1, began one of London Transport's most famous classes.

By then its engine had been increased to 9.6-litre capacity by increasing the bore size from 115mm to 120mm, retaining 142mm stroke and having the pot-cavity combustion system still favoured by LPTB, this version being put into production as type A185. The main new feature of the RT chassis was compressed-air operation of the brakes and the preselective gearbox, though there was extensive redesign, right down to the frame. Outwardly, there was a new lower bonnet line and, within, a flexible engine mounting reduced the noise and vibration transmitted to passengers. The LPTB placed orders for production batches of this model, at that stage generally described as the Regent RT, and included in the O661 series of chassis numbers despite its almost complete redesign as compared to the basic model.

From about mid-1939, AEC engineers were favouring general use of the toroidal system and, in addition to the adoption of the A173 as standard, Regents with toroidal versions of the A180 engine were being built for various north of England municipal fleets.

Above:
To replace most of the original Green Line Regals of 1930-1, London Transport ordered 266 Regal chassis with a newly introduced version of the 8.8-litre engine using the Leyland-style pot-cavity direct-injection system, designated A180. No fan was fitted and the water pump was repositioned, allowing the forward projection of the radiator usual with the 8.8 to be almost eliminated. It was thus possible to seat up to 34 passengers with adequate leg-room, as on the later examples, including T619, seen here in September 1938 at Eccleston Bridge, Victoria, within a few weeks of entering service. *G. H. F. Atkins*

Below:
The A180 direct-injection engine was chosen by several municipal operators for Regent buses in the 1938-40 period, but in such cases the usual 8.8-litre radiator position was retained. Salford Corporation was one such operator, its earlier examples being built with pot-cavity engines and the later ones of the toroidal type. The vehicle seen here was delivered early in 1939 and had a Park Royal metal-framed body seating 48 passengers, this capacity being standard in the fleet at the time. *AEC/Author's collection*

Top:
On 13 July 1939, London Transport revealed its new pride and joy: the first of a new breed of double-deck bus, RT1, seen here at The Spaniards Inn, Hampstead Heath, during a press run. The chassis was almost completely redesigned despite still being included in the Regent O661 chassis number series, and a new design of body, built by LPTB at Chiswick, set styling standards altered only slightly on the last RT buses completed 15 years later. *The Omnibus Society*

Above:
A prototype underfloor-engined single-decker chassis with the experimental project number A917/2 was built in 1939 and bodied by Weymann for service in Montreal just as war broke out. After the war, it was returned to Southall, being used in the development of the Regal Mark IV. *AEC/Author's collection*

7. AEC at War Again

In the period from 1938, as the political situation in Europe worsened, there was a revival in the development and production of military vehicles at AEC. Hence the immediate effect of the outbreak of war with Germany on 3 September 1939 was more to give such work top priority rather than any abrupt change of role. A clue to how it had been intermingled with AEC's more usual output is given by the issue of engine type numbers A183 and A184 (which came between what can be described loosely as the pre-production and production RT engine designs, A182 and A185) to a pair of '6.6-litre' six-cylinder Comet-head engines for use in tanks.

At first civilian production did not stop, even though it was delayed. Delivery of the chassis for the first production batch of 150 RT buses for London Transport began a month after the declaration of war and, after bodying at Chiswick, the first few entered service in January 1940. The chassis delivery was completed in May but the last bus did not enter service until February 1942. This was partly because of problems experienced with the air-pressure system, but the war did allow time to put this right. Indeed the perseverance of engineers at both Chiswick and Southall at a time when aerial attacks on London were frequent and the war situation was worsening laid the foundations for the widespread adoption of air operation of brakes on the heavier classes of British commercial vehicles in later years. Production

of AEC bus chassis for other users continued until the fateful summer of 1940 — a few were even exported — but then virtually ceased as Britain faced a threat of invasion, though limited civilian goods output continued. The service depot alongside the Southall factory was hit in one of the 1940 air raids but, rather surprisingly, the works itself escaped significant damage throughout the war, though it was among the Luftwaffe's targets.

Part of the early military output was of the Marshal 6x4 model with four-cylinder petrol engine, much as designed in response to an already-dated War Department specification of 1931, its rear bogie retaining the semi-floating axles of that period. Of the 934 built, 600 left the factory in 1939-41.

Belonging to a more up-to-date military era was the Matador 4x4 model adopted by the Army as its standard medium gun tractor. The combination of four-wheel drive and large-section tyres gave good cross-country capability,

Below:
The Marshal was designed to meet a War Department specification of 1931, not initially with much response, but it was put into larger-scale production in 1939-40 in the form shown here. The small hubs of the semi-floating rear axles remained as a give-away of the date of the design and, even at that earlier date, the Army was oddly conservative in its preference for an open-topped cab. *Imperial War Museum*

Above:
Development of engines for use in tanks had begun before the war. The Matilda tank built by the Vulcan Foundry had a pair of AEC '6.6-litre' six-cylinder Comet-head oil engines, basically similar to the unit used in the Regal Mark II.
Ian Allan Library

Right:
The paired engines, types A183 and A184, for the Matilda tank had injection pumps and other items arranged in the space between them to allow access for maintenance when installed in the tank hull. Some of these engines, modified to direct-injection, were later converted for bus use by the Northern General Transport Co Ltd, those with injection pumps on the right being used for some of that concern's own-make NGT side-engined buses previously having American Hercules petrol engines.
AEC/Author's Collection

and in due course this led to wider applications, including use by the Royal Air Force. The chassis, with design features traceable to Hardy and FWD origins, had been developed in 1938 and was thus already a production model when war came, though the numbers ordered were soon greatly increased.

The type number O853 also gave a clue to the Hardy link, following on from 852 which had been used for the railcars. The use of the model name Matador for this application was at first surprising as, before the war, it had been applied to civilian goods models of very different design. The standard engine was basically the toroidal 7.7, though installation differences caused this application to be A187 rather than A173. For a minority of applications, including early RAF examples, petrol engines were

required and a 110mm bore six-cylinder unit based on the A162 but designated A193 was made available from 1940.

The success of this model was such that it remained in production right through to the end of the war, the numbers built being comparable to those of the Y-type of the previous world war. When output from the military contracts ceased in November 1945, the total had reached

9,620. In the event, there proved to be renewed demand postwar, both civilian — the model proved almost ideally suited to timber haulage — and military, and batches continued to be built until as late June 1959, by which date the total reached 10,401.

Model 854 took the same concept to six-wheel-drive (6x6) by adding a Marshal-type rear bogie at the rear of a design otherwise very like the 4x4 Matador, though in this case no name was applied. The development for the RAF of four-engined bombers, with fuel tank capacity of over 2,000gal created an urgent need for tankers to refuel them swiftly when the aircraft were at dispersal points, possibly on soft ground and an all-wheel-drive 2,500gal refuelling tanker was needed.

The 854 was designed and put into production with great urgency, at first with petrol engine and requiring a special broad radiator to keep this cool under continuous pumping while stationary. From about 1942, however, the 7.7-litre oil engine was adopted (A196 in this application), the model number becoming O854. A total of 1,891 were built between 1940 and 1944.

AEC also built nearly 4,000 engines for tanks. Work on this went back to 1937, when a petrol engine based on the 'old-style' A165 8.8-litre diesel but opened out to 9.6-litre size was developed as the A179 for the Valentine tank — by early wartime there were A189 petrol and A190 Ricardo-head diesel versions. However, when the demand for armoured fighting vehicles was acute, G. J. Rackham,

again serving on a tank design committee, saw a place for an armoured car, more nimble than a tank on suitable terrain, yet big enough to carry an effective gun. At first he failed to persuade officialdom but AEC built a mock-up as a private venture and this was slipped into a display of military vehicles to be attended by the Prime Minister, Mr Winston Churchill — the outcome was official backing.

The first production type, the O855, known as the Mark I, was based on similar mechanical units to the Matador O853, though with rear-mounted 7.7 toroidal engine (type A195 in this form); 119 were built in 1942. A need for more power led to the O856, with an engine, type A197, evident-ly based on the old-style A165 8.8-litre crankcase but opened out to 9.6-litre capacity and with Ricardo Comet head giving up to 158bhp, this going into the O856 armoured car, of which 500 were built. It was known as the Mark II and then the Mark III with a larger six-pounder gun.

Meanwhile a brief return to bus chassis production came towards the end of 1941, when AEC was allowed to build 92 Regent chassis from stock parts to a fairly basic specification, with A173 7.7-litre engine and crash gearbox. Most entered service in 1942 with bodies to the 'utility' specification of the time.

After that, civilian chassis production ceased until 1945, but quite large numbers of 7.7-litre engines were supplied to other manufacturers permitted to build goods or bus chassis from 1943 — Daimler took A173 engines for its CWA6 wartime model while a new variant, type A202, with installation details to make it readily fitted in place of the Gardner 5LW, was supplied to Atkinson and Maudslay for lorries and to Bristol for buses. In addition, quite a number of operators took A173 engines to convert older buses or lorries, mainly but not exclusively AEC, and many operators had Comet-head engines converted to direct injection. Among the more notable cases was London Transport, which converted all the A165 Comet-head 8.8-litre engines in LT-class buses to pot-cavity direct injection; hence most of the buses of this class had 'pot' engines by 1943. By the end of the war, direct-injection AEC engines, mainly toroidal, greatly outnumbered the Comet types.

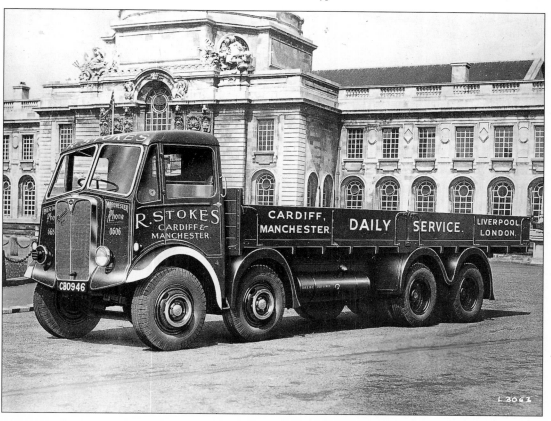

Top:
AEC's own transport fleet was expanded by the addition of five Mammoth Major eight-wheelers in January-March 1941. They had extra fuel tanks giving an 86gal total capacity and, with their direct-injection engines, a range of approximately 1,000 miles was said to be possible. Saving fuel, which was all imported, was always a priority in wartime, and one of these vehicles is seen later that year carrying four sets of paired engines for tanks as well as towing a 661T-type trolley-bus which had been bodied by Weymann for the Notts & Derby fleet. *AEC/Author's collection*

Above:
This Regal II was originally purchased in 1938 by J. Wainwright of Birmingham for specialised haulage, such as bulk delivery of motorcycles. Though it built up a substantial mileage, it did not prove entirely satisfactory and was taken in part-exchange against a new standard Regal, and was then added to AEC's own expanded wartime fleet. It is seen before setting out from Southall with a mixed load of items for service depots and customers. *AEC/Author's collection*

Above:
The rapid expansion of the Royal Air Force's fleet of four-engined bombers produced an urgent need for a fleet of 2,500gal petrol tankers that could cope with what might be soft and uneven ground in order to reach the aircraft at the dispersal points. The six-wheel-drive (6x6) model 854 that resulted could be regarded as a marriage of the Matador O853 and the Marshal 644, using the latter's rear bogie. At first the RAF favoured petrol engines and the example shown is believed to be an early one, with radiator similar to the O853 pattern. *AEC/Author's collection*

Below:
Rapid refuelling was essential at typical RAF bomber bases when up to 57 aircraft, each liable to require almost a full tanker-load, had to be made ready for each night's action by six 854-type tankers. Here a Halifax is being refuelled. *Imperial War Museum*

Right:
With all-wheel drive, and suitably low gearing via main and auxiliary gearboxes, the 854 could also act as a tractor. A Sunderland four-engined flying boat is towed ashore at a Scottish coastal command base. This vehicle had the much broader radiator standardised for a time for this model. *AEC/Author's collection*

Below:
Bus production virtually stopped after the war situation worsened in 1940, but building of what were nicknamed 'unfrozen' chassis from parts in stock was allowed in 1941-2 and allocated on a basis of need. Many of these 92 Regent chassis went to fleets where AEC buses were rare. Edinburgh Corporation had none newer than 1929 until two unfrozen Regents with Park Royal bodies to the wartime utility specification then in force arrived late in 1941. Near-normal peacetime livery helped their appearance. By that date many buses, new and old, were in wartime grey of varying shades. *AEC/Author's collection*

Top:
The AEC armoured car began as a private venture. This picture dating from May 1943 shows an O856 of the Mark II type. It was based on axles similar to the Matador O853 but had an engine mounted at the rear derived from the prewar 8.8-litre Comet-head engine, opened out to 9.6-litre capacity and giving up to 158bhp. This version had a two-pounder gun which proved inadequate against German armoured vehicles of the period but the Mark III had a much more effective six-pounder. *AEC/Ian Allan Library*

Above:
The armoured command vehicle, intended for use as a head-quarters base in the field of battle, was based on a Matador O853 chassis, this picture dating from May 1943. It could hardly be called pretty, but that was the last consideration as preparations were being made for the assault on Europe the following year. *AEC/Ian Allan Library*

Above:

Although AEC was required to devote all its output of new vehicles to military purposes during much of the war, it was possible to supply conversion engines for existing vehicles. One of the most interesting examples was the first Regent chassis, No 661001, which had begun life with a petrol engine and a Short Bros double-deck bus body early in 1929 as a demonstrator. It was registered by AEC as MT 2114 although sold to Halifax Corporation in 1930. By wartime it had been rebodied as a furniture van for A. Batty Ltd of Bradford and in May 1943 received an A173 7.7-litre oil engine — a radiator of late 1930s style had also been fitted. *AEC/Author's collection*

Below:

Under wartime Government schemes, AEC engines were also allocated to other vehicle makers. Daimler, which had standardised on Gardner engines in the later 1930s, was switched to the AEC A173 7.7-litre engine for production of its wartime CWA6 bus chassis. This example with Duple utility body was one of those supplied to London Transport, which built up a fleet of 269 CWA6s delivered between 1944 and 1946. With fluid flywheels and preselective gearboxes, they offered performance characteristics broadly similar to the standard STL-class Regents. *Ian Allan Library*

8. Into the Mark III Era

When the six years of war in Europe ended in May 1945, the pent-up demand for both bus and lorry chassis was huge. AEC was able to standardise to a far greater degree than in 1939, six-cylinder direct-injection oil engines becoming universal for production models, with no four-cylinder or petrol options. On the other hand, export and dimensional variants soon began to multiply.

The 7.7-litre A173 engine, together with 'crash' gearbox, was used for the initial postwar range. The Regent double-decker chassis, designated O661/20, was almost identical to that of the 'unfrozen' Regent buses of 1942, except that its brake system was of the vacuum triple-servo type instead of vacuum-hydraulic. Even so, it was called the Regent II. Briefly, the corresponding single-deck model was similarly named Regal II until someone remembered the quite different O862 chassis which had that title up to 1939 and the O662/20 was hastily retitled Regal I.

A total of 695 Regent II and 1,665 Regal I chassis (50 of the former and 444 of the latter for export) were built between August 1945 and the end of 1947. These brought the totals of the Regent and Regal in the 661 and 662 series built since the beginning of these models in 1929 to 7,892 and 5,286 respectively. Bodybuilding delays meant that quite a few of the postwar examples did not enter service until 1948 and in a few cases as late as 1950.

Below:
The urgent need for new civilian vehicles in 1945 made it simpler to begin with models very similar to those previously in production. The title Regent II was applied to the postwar model O661/20, very like the 1941-2 version. The effect was heightened in early cases where Park Royal built the bodywork as that firm continued building what was virtually its wartime design well into 1946 — the example shown was supplied to Leicester Corporation in January 1946. *R. A. Mills*

Above:
Nearly half the 645 home-market Regent II buses received metal-framed bodywork to this design, built by Weymann (or in the case of 100 for Liverpool, based on Weymann frames) between December 1945 and 1948. Shown here is one of eight dating from November 1946 in the Midland General fleet. The smooth contours of the body gave an impression of refinement not quite matched by the chassis with its rigid mounting of the 7.7-litre engine. *G. H. F. Atkins*

Below:
London Transport added 50 Regal I buses as well as 20 Regent II, all with Weymann bodywork, to its fleet in late 1945 and 1946, numbering them in its T and STL classes respectively, though the specifications, with crash gearbox and 'provincial' body styles, were far removed from its previous standards. The Regals were used for suburban services, T743 being seen in New Malden. *F. G. Reynolds*

On the goods side, the Monarch now also had the 7.7-litre engine, the chassis being designated O346S, the suffix indicating 'solo' as opposed to the revived civilian Matador O346, which differed in having an auxiliary gearbox and brake gear allowing for operation with a trailer. The total of such Matador models added 486 to the prewar total of 286 for the O346 and 346 types, while that of the Monarch O346S, built between 1945 and 1947, was 471. All these passenger and goods models in the immediate postwar range could be described as down-to-earth no-frills vehicles, well suited to the needs of the times. They were seen as a stopgap for the new Mark III range largely powered by the 9.6-litre engine, though that was adopted from 1946 for the postwar O366/20 and O386/20 six- and eight-wheeled Mammoth Major types.

A model cutting across this tidy uniformity just after the war was the O858 6x6 bonneted tractor, originally designed as part of the wartime military series and having a Ricardo Comet III 9.6-litre engine derived from the prewar A165 unit and developing 150bhp. It was adopted by the Iraq Petroleum Co Ltd, mainly to haul pipe-carrying semi-trailers. A total of 95 were built during 1946-8.

The description 'Regent Mark III' had begun to be used in wartime AEC advertisements conveying postwar plans, illustrated by a picture of one of the London RT buses placed in service in 1940. They referred to its main special features, such as the 9.6-litre rubber-mounted engine and air-pressure operation of the brakes and preselective gearbox. One such bus, RT19, had been borrowed back by AEC when almost new until 1942 for use as a demonstrator, visiting at least 22 provincial operators, many of them later to become major buyers of Regent III buses.

At that stage, the impression was given that the latter would differ only in minor details from the RT, just as had been so with the ST and STL in relation to earlier generations of standard Regent. For the first postwar deliveries beginning at the end of 1946 that was so, but it became clear from 1947 that the standard provincial Regent III was not to have the low bonnet level of the RT, though a new frontal design made it readily distinguishable from the Regent II or earlier types. Even so, there was more in common between the RT and provincial versions than superficial, or even the quite numerous practical, differences suggested, as many major parts were common to both.

The postwar RT and other Regent III buses with 9.6-litre engines (now with the toroidal form of direct injection, a feature adopted for RT19 before its wartime demonstration tour) shared the same chassis number series, beginning at O961001. This continued even when a revised model numbering system introduced in January 1948 caused the standard provincial version to become 9612E. The 'O' prefix signifying 'oil engine', superfluous by then, was dropped for almost all AEC models except the London RT chassis; henceforth 'O961' signified this type only.

Provincial Regent III chassis had briefly been classified O961/2 in AEC's previous drawing office system, and the fourth figure in the new designation thus similarly indicated 'series 2', the suffix letter 'E' signifying the epicyclic Wilson gearbox. A minority of operators, most notably at that stage the BET group, preferred the crash gearbox and vacuum brakes, so 9612A indicated a

Top:
The Monarch became a six-cylinder model postwar, when the A173 7.7-litre unit became the smallest-capacity engine in the production range. This one with livestock-carrying body was supplied to J. Filbee of Tilehurst, near Reading, in 1948. It is posed with the self-conscious-looking owner at AEC's works gates in Windmill Lane, Southall. *AEC/Ian Allan Library*

Above:
With the war over, 'Matador' once gain meant the standard two-axle goods model designed for possible trailer haulage. These two, with platform bodywork, for G. L. Baker Ltd of London E14 were also posed at the works entrance but with the camera looking towards the Iron Bridge which runs diagonally across the Uxbridge Road, then carrying AEC advertisements. Most AEC goods vehicles of that period received the rather stylish AEC design of cab shown, built by various bodybuilders. *AEC/Ian Allan Library*

Above:
The Regent Mark III was expected to be as closely related to the RT as the prewar Regents for general sale had been to the STL, and at first it seemed as if this would be so. Aberdeen Corporation was one of a number of operators receiving buses based on RT-style chassis in the winter of 1946-7, the example seen here entering service in December 1946, one of a batch of 10. They had Weymann bodies to a four-bay version of that firm's standard design of the time. *AEC/Ian Allan Library*

Left:
The impression made on London's streets by the growing numbers of gleaming new RT buses was quite dramatic. This picture of RT772 taken when newly arrived at Dalston garage for service on route 9 in August 1948 conveys something of their glamorous looks — by that date about 50 were entering service per month. This vehicle was bodied by Park Royal but identical bodies were being built by Weymann, although at the time the latter, painted green rather than red, were being delivered to country garages, as was often the case in later years. *Ian Allan Library*

9.6-litre model having these features — 'A', rather irrationally, signified 'AEC gearbox' even though the epicyclic boxes, too, were made by AEC. There was also a more limited demand for a 7.7-litre crash-gearbox version with the new frame, axles appearance and flexible engine mounting, this becoming 6811A.

Equivalent Regal single-deck models and designations were used, though here there was no version with RT-style

bonnet and hence the Regal equivalent to a 9612E was a 9621E, itself apt to cause confusion if the digits became accidentally transposed. In practice, the largest home-market Regal III demand was for the 7.7-litre version, of which early examples were designated O682 before switching to 6821A.

The Regal III proved to be primarily an export model and AEC took the bold step of not only offering left-hand steering but producing an almost complete mirror-image 9.6-litre engine and chassis, model O963, later 9631E. Good accessibility of items needing servicing or overhaul attention was always regarded as important at AEC, reflecting the firm's origins and continuing close association with people who ran buses. Designations of

the 9.6-litre engine became quite complex, but the main variants were A204 for the RT version; A206, goods; A207, left-hand (goods or passenger); and A208 'provincial' passenger. These latter three, all of which had oil-bath air cleaners which would not fit under the RT bonnet, moved on to A216, A217 and A218 when a revised water flow was adopted.

In the aftermath of the war, the Government put great emphasis on exports to earn much-needed foreign currency, and the left-hand Regal proved very successful, notably in South America. There was more limited demand for left-hand-drive double-deckers and the 9631E chassis was used for these also, even though usually then described as Regent III — those sent for service in Lisbon, some of which covered well over a million miles on arduous routes, became particularly famous. It is significant that the left-hand-drive O963/9631E series models outnumbered both the home and export right-hand O962/9621E.

However, the main output was of Regent III models for use in Britain and in particular the London RT. Plans for large-scale output had been made while the war was still raging and chassis production began early in 1946, but the LPTB decided upon a jig-built form of body construction derived from aircraft practice and it was not until May 1947 that the first two entered service, one each from the two main bodybuilders, Park Royal and Weymann, though to identical design, being outwardly quite similar to the 1939 original. Once under way, however, the numbers grew rapidly and during the peak year, 1950, 1,056 entered service. By early 1949, a start had been made on the second 1,000 chassis, being built at a rate of over a dozen a week, and when production ended in 1954, some

4,674 of the postwar RT chassis had been built, the fleet number series begun in 1939 reaching RT4825.

The postwar RT was remarkably standardised, with only minor changes throughout its production. The provincial Regent III was not quite so much so and the increase of the legal length limit to 27ft in 1950 led to the 9613E and 9613A versions — there had been an 8ft-wide option from 1947.

In 1946, it was decided that trolleybus and railcar

Right:
The Regal Mark III, with 9.6-litre engine, preselective gearbox and air brakes as standard, sold well in left-hand-drive form. South America was a particularly strong market, and this scene in Buenos Aires, Argentina, in November 1948 shows the inauguration of a new state-owned bus undertaking, Empresa Nacional '17 Octobre', using 35 ACLO Regal IIIs with Saunders bodywork diverted from a fleet of 50 ordered by Buenos Aires Transport Board.
Ian Allan Library

manufacture would be the subject of a joint venture with Leyland, the British United Traction Co Ltd, though in practice the home-market BUT trolleybus range was of AEC design, derived from the Mark III passenger range, the best known types being the 9611T and 9641T two- and three-axle models. Much of the BUT railcar manufacture, which for a time was mainly for Irish railways, also continued to be under AEC's wing.

Revised goods models had emerged more gradually in the immediate postwar era. The first goods Mark IIIs were two-axle types retaining vacuum brakes: the Monarch O345 (soon becoming 3451, in essentials much as built from 1945 and together adding a further 1,418 examples) and Matador 3471, the latter also now having the 9.6-litre engine and soon moving on to 3472 with a new five-speed gearbox. Then the Mammoth Major Mark III appeared, with 9.6 engine, the five-speed gearbox and air-pressure brakes, designated 3671 or 3871. The eight-wheel model was to prove the most popular of the Mark III goods range, with 3,197 right-hand examples having been built when production ceased in 1960, but there were also 2,024 right-hand six-wheelers.

For export, there were bonneted versions of the four- and six-wheel 9.6-litre models (the initial model number becoming 2 instead of the 3 which still signified forward-control) and left-hand-drive versions of all 9.6 models (the third digit then becoming 8 instead of 7). Adding further to the permutations, the six- and eight-wheel models were available with single-axle drive or three alternative forms of double-drive, adding H, K or M to the designations.

To meet the demand for more power, a new 11.3-litre 150bhp engine appeared in 1949 and became available on the heavier-duty models, notably export and goods types. It was derived from the 9.6-litre engine, with bore increased to 130mm, yet installation and many parts were unchanged — quite an achievement in compact design.

Although the AEC range of this period had numerous variations, a great deal of it was based on parts of standardised design, and a wide variety of needs could be met by assembling the appropriate combination of production items, an approach to design which was characteristic of the Rackham era.

After the collapse of ADC in 1928, AEC had stayed clear of mergers although there had been various proposals, and even the 1946 link with Leyland in the BUT trolleybus and railcar business was deliberately limited in scope. However, in 1948 two old-established commercial vehicle makers, Crossley Motors Ltd and the Maudslay Motor Co Ltd, decided to sell out, and this led to a change of title from the Associated Equipment Co Ltd to Associated

Above:
The announcement in June 1949 of an 11.3-litre engine having much in common, including its external dimensions, with the 9.6-litre unit was quite an achievement — the initial production version was type A214. It gave 150bhp at 1,800rpm — this view shows an early example with fluid flywheel and the axial form of flexible mounting, suitable for a right-hand-drive passenger application, probably an export Regal III. *AEC/Ian Allan Library*

Commercial Vehicles Ltd which took effect from 1 October 1948. From that date, ACV became a holding company for the AEC, Crossley and Maudslay manufacturing concerns — the full official title of the AEC manufacturing business simultaneously changed to AEC Ltd. For some years, Crossley and Maudslay continued to produce their own designs of vehicle, though Maudslay had standardised on AEC engines since wartime. The bodybuilding concern, Park Royal Vehicles Ltd, of which Charles H. Roe Ltd was already a subsidiary, also came into the ACV group in 1949.

An important new addition to the range announced in 1949 was the Regal Mark IV, quite different from the pre-war Regal 4, being an underfloor-engined single-deck model using a horizontal (A219) version of the 9.6-litre engine together with other units similar in specification to the Regal III, though with a set-back front axle to allow the entrance to be positioned in front of it. There had been a prototype chassis of similar layout built in 1939 and sent to Canada, this being returned after the war and again run by the Experimental Department.

The initial standard Regal IV was type 9821E, though by far the largest order was for 700 basically similar chassis designated 9821LT which formed London Transport's RF class, placed in service between 1951 and 1953. All but the first 25 were of 30ft length, this having become permissible from mid-1950 for two-axle single-deckers in place of the previous 27ft 6in; 8ft width was also allowed, though not taken up for the RF class. Other home market sales were largely for use as coaches but again there was a strong export element, notably the left-hand 9831E and subsequent variants. A prototype Regent IV was built in 1950, differing from the single-decker in not having the set-back front axle but it did not go into production.

Left:
To augment deliveries, London Transport added further body-builders to its suppliers. This convoy of RT buses led by RT1298 crossing the Menai Bridge in January 1950 was being delivered from Saunders Engineering & Shipyard Ltd, based at Beaumaris, Anglesey. Saunders was producing 250 bodies to the same outline as those by Park Royal or Weymann, though based on its own design of framing. The London fleet put 1,056 new RT buses into service in 1950, the peak year for deliveries. *Saro/Ian Allan Library*

Above:
Bonneted goods models continued to be favoured for some export markets and this Matador 2482 left-hand-drive tractor unit is typical of the units apt to be seen in AEC's works yard awaiting shipment in the late 1940s or early 1950s after being fitted with cabs, although many such vehicles had the upper part of the cab detached to reduce shipping costs.
AEC/Ian Allan Library

Below:
The takeover of Crossley in 1948 was followed by a period during which it continued to produce its own designs of vehicles as a member of the ACV group, alongside AEC. Here a Crossley SD42/7 with Metalcraft body dating from March 1950 of Cooper of Oakengates, Shropshire, is seen with an AEC Regal III 96ZIE model with Strachans body of similar age of Slatter of Long Handborough, Oxfordshire. They are parked outside Wembley Stadium in May 1950. *Ian Allan Library*

Left:
Maudslay was one of the makers which began using AEC engines in wartime, continuing this policy for most of its postwar range. A merger was an obvious step, but here, too, production of Maudslay-designed chassis continued for a time. This Meritor eight-wheeler van was supplied to Holdsworth & Burrill, by then part of the state-owned British Transport Commission empire, in 1949. *Author's collection*

Below left:
The last major new model of the Rackham era to be put into production was the underfloor-engined Regal Mark IV. This prototype with one of three pre-production chassis, U137525, and Duple coach body of 1950 is seen undergoing testing on the Belgian pavé surface at the Motor Industry Research Association proving ground at Lindley, near Nuneaton. The coach was later sold to Berry of Bradford-on-Tone, being registered NYD 509. *Ian Allan Library*

Below:
The fleet of AEC buses operated in Lisbon by the concern best known simply as Carris was famous for its longevity. This Regal III 9631E dating from 1948 was still coping with the hilly 37 route to St George's Castle in 1982. *David Stuttard*

9. The 1950s — A Decade of Change

G. J. Rackham retired in June 1950, having been Chief Engineer at AEC for 22 years. He was succeeded by George Robinson, who had been his deputy since they were both at Leyland. For several years the sense of continuity was strong, and many Rackham-era units or components were still in use into the 1960s.

However, another influence on engineering policy arose from the appointment of A. J. Romer as Managing Director in August 1950, for he was a qualified engineer and had been General Manager of the bus chassis manufacturing works of the Bristol concern since 1936. He had been involved in the development of the Lodekka low-floor double-decker, of which two prototypes had been completed just before his move to AEC.

What might have been taken for a change of direction was the appearance of synchromesh versions of the Regent III and the Regal IV. Yet AEC had built modest numbers of such gearboxes in the late 1930s, when this was virtually unheard of on the heavier types of commercial vehicle even though well established on cars, putting them out in Regent buses for trial in several city fleets without publicity. No further action was taken in this direction until 1950. Leyland had made a synchromesh gearbox standard for its new PD2 version of the Titan from 1947, this being the most direct competitor to the Regent III. Crossley had offered one from about the same

time, and in fact some of the latter were fitted to 10 Regent and 20 Regal III buses for the Trent fleet in 1950.

A new AEC-designed synchromesh gearbox was first introduced on the Regal IV, model 9821S, and then the Regent III, model 9613S. Both had synchromesh on all four forward ratios but a clearly recognisable AEC sound, if anything a little louder than from the previous 'crash' box, was given by the straight-cut gear teeth.

ACV group policy led to the phasing out of the Crossley and Maudslay concerns' own designs of chassis but, for a period during the 1950s, models of standard AEC design but badged as products of those companies were offered. This seems to have been largely a ploy to boost the group's representation at Commercial Motor Shows, the exhibits in question quite often reverting to

Below:
Scottish Omnibuses Ltd continued to use the SMT fleetname throughout the 1950s despite the change of company name after it became state-owned in 1949. A new fleet of AEC Regal IV coaches for its Edinburgh-London service arrived in 1951, the first vehicle being posed by the Forth Bridge immediately after delivery in April. They were on 9821E-type chassis with epicyclic gearboxes and had Alexander bodywork with spacious seating for only 30 passengers and a toilet compartment. *Ian Allan Library*

AEC badges before delivery. However, some were permanent, notably a batch of nine Maudslay Regent IIIs for Coventry, and the Post Office was among users of goods models badged as Maudslay, while Maudslay fire engine versions of the Regent III were built for Merryweather. Somewhat confusingly, assembly of standard Mammoth Major chassis was largely transferred to Maudslay's works at Alcester for some years, but almost all of these bore AEC badges.

However, an addition to AEC's Mark III goods range was a twin-steering six-wheeler, a type found in Maudslay's own previous range in the form of the Mustang — the new model used AEC units but its design had been carried out at Maudslay. The name Majestic was

revived for it, the main model number being 3511, of which 54 were built.

Of much greater importance in production terms were the O859 6x4 and O860 6x6 Militant models introduced in 1952 and built mainly for the Army. They were introduced in response to a military specification, having the 11.3-litre engine and axles similar to the O858 but with forward-control — a total of 3,200 was built up to 1964.

Below:
Synchromesh gearboxes first appeared as a catalogued option among AEC models on the underfloor-engined Regal IV in response to pressure from the BET group of operating companies, among which City of Oxford Motor Services Ltd

was prominent in this respect. Here the first of six Regal IV model 9821S models with Willowbrook 42-seat bodywork is seen at AEC in May 1952.
E. J. Smith/Author's collection

Below:
Park Royal adopted a very RT-like outline for its own metal-framed body design for other chassis from late 1950. This example on the then new 27ft version of the Regent III chassis was a demonstrator completed in September of that year. It was painted in a Southdown-like green and cream livery, though, being a 9613E model, its preselective gearbox was unlikely to have appealed to that company. It was registered SMU 194 and was sold to D. Jones of Port Talbot in April 1952. *PRV/Author's collection*

Top:
Increasingly, Crossley and Maudslay were losing their separate identities as vehicle makers. This Regal IV, of standard 9821E design, was the first to be badged as a Maudslay and was given the chassis number M9821E10001. Initially, it was described as a Marathon IV, though later such vehicles were simply 'Maudslay Regal IV' — there were to be eight in all, dating from 1951-2. Its Gurney Nutting body seated 35 in a 'dining car' layout and it was supplied to F. A. Need, Kildare St Garage, of Longton, Stoke-on-Trent. *ACV/Ian Allan Library*

Above:
A more substantial Maudslay involvement in design occurred with the development of a twin-steering six-wheeled goods model, a type which had not been offered hitherto by AEC. It employed standard AEC units for the most part but the brake system was of the vacuum-hydraulic type, unlike any other AEC model of that period. This photograph is thought to show the prototype, with a radiator bearing a Maudslay badge and a Monarch script title — the production AEC-badged models offered from 1951 were given the model name Majestic and the type number 3511, having 9.6-litre engines. *Ian Allan Library*

The wartime Matador O853 was also revived and built in modest numbers — its total reached 10,401 when the last were built in 1959.

A major development in 1953 was the introduction of a new medium-weight range, bringing AEC's products into a lighter class than its existing models. This work was in the charge of R. A. (Bob) Fryars, who had risen within the firm to Assistant Chief Engineer; he was to become Chief Engineer in 1960.

Also new was a model designation system using mainly letters, often the initial of the word they conveyed — thus 'M' signified medium-weight, 'G' goods, 'U' underfloor-engined passenger, 'R' right-hand, 'L' left-hand. To indicate brake systems, 'V' signified vacuum; 'A' air-pressure and 'H' hydraulic, though this last could imply a system used with a servo or a power-hydraulic system. On passenger models, the exception was the one feature hitherto signified by letter, the transmission system, which

Below:
At the September 1952 Earls Court Show, a Regent III for Devon General was exhibited. The chassis had what was generally called a 'new look' front, to a Birmingham City Transport design, while the Weymann body was to a new design, called the Aurora. As built, the chassis was of type 9613A, with crash gearbox, but a prototype synchromesh gearbox was fitted before the bus entered service, effectively becoming type 9613S. The body design was not put into production and the vehicle remained unique.
AEC/Ian Allan Library

switched to numbers, 2 signifying an epicyclic gearbox, 3 synchromesh and 4 constant-mesh. On goods chassis, a numeral indicated the number of wheels (counting twin-tyre assemblies as one wheel).

The power units for the new range had their roots in the A172 engine used in the Regal Mark II of 1936, inheriting its wet-liner construction, though with toroidal direct injection, and the smaller of the two had the same 105mm bore and 130mm stroke, with swept volume of 6.75 litres. An alternative version, soon established as the more popular, had 112mm bore, which gave a true 7.7-litre capacity, the latter having obvious possibilities for confusion with the A173 unit, then being phased out. However, the new engines also had new-style designations, prefixed AV if vertical for use in front-engined models and AH if horizontal. The capacity was expressed in cubic inches, in line with a national convention of the time, and the engines were thus AV410 or AV470 as used in the new-generation Mercury goods model GM4RA etc, or AH410 or AH470 if horizontal.

AEC had got as far as producing a prototype lighter goods chassis with semi-forward control in 1939 and the first prototype for the new-generation model was of similar layout. However, production models, which revived the name Mercury, were of forward-control type, though with the driving position set far enough back for the gear lever to act directly on the gearbox — the standard cab had a bulbous panel below the vee windscreen. Initially, it was of 12-ton gross weight

capacity but later in the 1950s, when it became legal to operate two-axle models at 14 tons, the Mercury Mark II, designated 2GM4RA, appeared — the use of a prefix number to indicate later versions became regular practice on other models in a similar way.

The Mercury sold in much larger numbers than any previous civilian AEC goods model — by December 1964, 9,239 right-hand examples had been sold, plus 510 of the left-hand GM4LA etc, these latter designated Monarch Mark V or VI; Mercury was by then well established in many overseas markets as a marque name for a mid-priced car made by the American Ford organisation. The Mustang name hitherto favoured by

Above:
Crossley was also involved in 'badge engineering' masquerades. This left-hand-drive Regal IV chassis being towed into Earls Court for the September 1954 Show was nominally of that make, at least for the duration of the exhibition. The standing steersman, cigarette dangling from his lips and helpers casually seated on the chassis would not be approved of in today's safety-conscious world.
Ian Allan Library

Below:
Argentina continued to be an important market. This ACLO Matador left-hand-drive tractor of Transportes Castella, of Buenos Aires, bore the words 'Chassis Ingles' proudly on its bonnet side panels — it was used with a 20-ton semi-trailer on a 350-mile run from Santa Fe to Buenos Aires carrying chickens and eggs. *AEC/Ian Allan Library*

Above:
The war in Korea brought a renewal of interest in military vehicles, including further construction of Matador O853 models, though in smaller numbers than in World War 2 — this chassis in standard postwar aluminium paint finish was built in response to a Ministry of Supply order and dated from November 1952. *ACV/Ian Allan Library*

Below:
A new generation of models designed for Army use began with the O859 6x4 model, of which the prototype was running by May 1951 — later it and the similar O860 6x6 version were given the name Militant. Both had the 11.3-litre engine, being built as general service lorries, conservatively rated in usual Army fashion at a 10-ton load capacity and with various specialised bodies, including this 2,500gal O859 fuel tanker dating from 1954. *Ian Allan Library*

Above:
London Transport continued to take delivery of new RT-type double-deckers until November 1954. The chassis specification was altered only in minor details throughout the postwar run of 4,674 chassis for operation in London. Seen here at Aldgate is RT4500, which entered service in July 1954 as one of a batch for Green Line service. The bodywork, refurbished for such duty, had been built by Park Royal in 1949, having been on one of the stopgap SRT conversions of prewar STL-type chassis to RT outline which proved unsatisfactory and were being withdrawn. *G. H. F. Atkins*

Left:
The introduction of the new-generation Mercury, type GM4RA, successfully took AEC into a fresh market sector, with the Leyland Comet as its most obvious competitor but also reaching towards the Bedford S-type or the Thames Trader. A rather bulbous profile was adopted, initially using quite a crude style of grille, with only the triangle badge as a clear indication of identity. This example entered service with Elsey and Bent Ltd of Peterborough in late 1954. *Ian Allan Library*

Maudslay was adopted from 1956 for an 18-ton gross, twin-steering, six-wheeler in this range, designated GM6RH, of which 350 were built in 1956-63. In 1961, a conventional 20-ton six-wheeler was added to the range, using the name Marshal, type GM6RHB, of which 990 were built by the end of 1964. There was even a medium-weight Matador Mark II, type 4GM4RA, a 4x4 version using the AV470 engine, though few were built.

The medium-weight underfloor-engined bus or coach chassis, of which type MU3RV with vacuum brakes was the most popular, revived another name of the past, Reliance. With typical bus body seating 44 or 45, the unladen weight was under 6 tons, nearly two tons less than most Regal IV models, giving useful fuel economy benefits, important when operators were beginning to be hit by falling demand for bus travel. There was also a semi-integral bus, type MC3RV, rather confusingly called the Monocoach, giving expectations of further weight saving. It had a special underframe designed to be built

into a completed bus body shell by Park Royal, though the latter also bodied some Reliance chassis and some Monocoaches were completed by others. Air-braked versions, MU3RA etc, were offered but were less common than on heavier-duty models.

The Reliance had broader appeal than the Regal IV, with 5,829 of the MU3RV and other right-hand models built between 1953 and the end of 1964, to which were added 763 of the left-hand types, MU3LA etc. The home-market version was supplied to a wide variety of operators, from major BET group companies for both bus and coach duties, including several firms not hitherto AEC users, such as Aldershot & District and East Kent, to independent coach operators, among whom it was the most popular underfloor-engined model of that period. Only a handful of Regal IVs were built for the home market after 1954, by which date a little under 1,500 had been sold in Britain, but it continued as a heavy-duty export model until 1960, some 752 of the left-hand versions being built, largely for South America, up to 1960.

The Monocoach proved to have a more limited appeal, though early users included Northern General Transport, Scottish Omnibuses and W. Alexander & Sons — 168 had been ordered in the 1954-5 period but then sales virtually collapsed in Britain, operators finding Reliance chassis with conventional bodies a better proposition, with no significant extra weight. However, a steadier export demand for the Monocoach came from Portugal where the UTIC organisation was expanding the market for AEC vehicles.

The situation with regard to double-deckers became quite complex, with a three-way split in development, reflecting different influences on AEC and some loss of

Above:
This picture taken in May 1954 shows the interior of a Park Royal cab on an early Mercury, giving a clear indication of the model's character, quite different from that of the existing AEC goods range. Note the gear lever, acting directly on the gear-box and hence requiring a rather awkward, almost vertical, action. *ACV/Ian Allan Library*

clarity in design policy. Continuity was evident in the new Regent V range introduced in 1954 to replace the Regent III, from which much of the design was inherited. Early publicity concentrated on the lightweight MD3RV version which had the AV470 engine, which found favour with some BET fleets for a time. There were also models with the A218 9.6-litre engine, the D3RV model having a synchromesh gearbox, chosen by several municipal fleets.

A new generation of Wilson gearbox was now offered, this eliminating the 'clutch' pedal (which was why '2' was chosen for this transmission in the type codes, signifying '2-pedal') and having direct selection of gears via an electrical system with a switch unit on the steering column, AEC's name for it being Monocontrol. The air-braked 9.6-litre Regent chassis thus fitted were designated D2RA, and an MD2RA model with the AV470 engine was added in 1956, being preferred by some municipalities. Monocontrol transmission was also offered for the Reliance but rarely specified at that stage.

Standard Regent V models had a new wide bonnet with front cowl concealing the radiator and bearing a grille

similar to that on Mercury models. Some late Regent III chassis had been fitted with the somewhat similar 'new look' front first produced on Birmingham Crossley buses and, rather confusingly, AEC also adopted the term 'new look' internally for its own concealed-radiator design. The option of the traditional-style radiator was continued for Regent V models and the combination of possibilities meant that the only significant point of difference of the 'heavyweight' synchromesh D3RV with old-style radiator from the 9613S version of the Regent III was the use of wider front springs.

In practice, there was some overlap and production of Regent III chassis continued until 1956. A total of approximately 8,633 of all variants had been built, though the main series of chassis of the O961, 9612E and related types with 9.6-litre engine and right-hand steering numbered 8,325.

The front-engined Regal III single-decker had also continued, though home sales had died out in favour of

Left:
The Regent Mark V appeared in September 1954, the first to be completed being this example of the light MD3RV version with Park Royal body, weighing just under 6½ tons unladen, exhibited at that year's Show with Crossley badges. It is seen here on demonstration duty with the Barton Transport fleet in March 1955, by which date it had acquired more appropriate AEC badges. *G. H. F. Atkins*

Below left:
The new style of grille as introduced for the Regent V was standardised for the Mercury. This demonstrator is seen in Purley while on road test for *Modern Transport* in August 1955. *Ian Allan Library*

Below:
The first Routemaster bus, RM1, developed jointly by London Transport, AEC and Park Royal, appeared on AEC's stand at the Commercial Motor Show in September 1954. By the time of the Lord Mayor's Show in November 1956, it had been modified, the radiator having been moved to the front from its original underfloor position, taking advantage of an increase in the legally permitted length. *AEC/Ian Allan Library*

underfloor-engined models after very limited numbers of 30ft versions were built post-1950. The type thereafter effectively became an export model — when production ended at the end of 1957, the most numerous version proved to be the left-hand 9631E etc, of which 1,765 had been built since 1946, largely for South America, notably Uruguay. There were 1,595 of the right-hand 9.6-litre types and 734 of the 6821A etc with 7.7-litre engines. Five examples of a chassis of similar layout, the Regal V, type S2LA, were built in 1959 for Luanda, Angola.

An additional option for the Regent V was the availability of the Gardner 6LW engine and a total of 120 such buses so powered were built in 1955-6 for the Glasgow, Aberdeen and Rochdale fleets, all with epicyclic gearboxes, mostly of the preselective type, the Glasgow and Aberdeen examples being unique among postwar AECs in combining this with vacuum brakes, being designated D2RV6G.

London Transport had adopted a more radical approach, deciding that a completely new type of double-decker, of integral construction, with aluminium structure, power-hydraulic brakes, independent front suspension and coil springs all round, would meet its requirements. A key part of the aim was to get weight down despite increasing seating capacity from the 56 of the RT to 64. It was christened the Routemaster and a prototype, RM1,

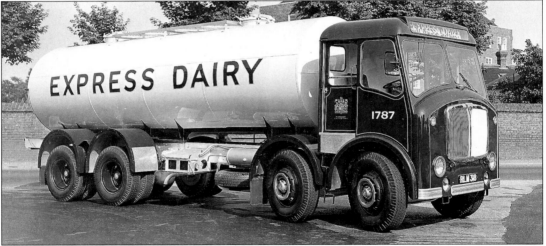

Top:
Fitting the new-style grille on the Mark III goods range doubtless seemed an obvious step, though its different proportions did not sit very happily on what was largely an unaltered cab. Park Royal, building eight to 10 cabs per week for AEC from autumn 1954, set up this comparison of a pair of Mammoth Majors, using a grille bearing a Regent title plate, evidently before regular output of the new option began in 1955. _PRV/Author's collection_

Above:
Rather better co-ordinated was this cab design using the new grille on a Mammoth Major Mark III tanker for Express Dairies dating from late 1955. Cab construction was still a matter for individual choice even though standardised cabs, largely by Park Royal, were becoming more common. _ACV/Author's collection_

developed jointly by LTE, AEC and Park Royal, was built for the 1954 Show. This had a 9.6-litre engine and was followed early in 1955 by RM2, originally with AV470 engine and having fully automatic transmission and power-assisted steering, the latter two items, rare on buses at that date, being adopted for production though this did not begin until 1958.

A third strand to AEC's efforts on double-deckers was the Bridgemaster. It too had integral construction, using a body structure of Park Royal design, and independent front suspension but in other ways was quite different from the Routemaster, the name referring to its low height despite having centre-gangway layout on both decks. A. J. Romer's influence and experience of the Bristol

Above:
The Regent continued to be AEC's best known bus. The increase in permitted length to 30ft for two-axle double-deckers operated in Britain in 1956 put the emphasis back towards the heavier duty models, with the introduction of new chassis to suit this need which had the A218 9.6-litre engine as standard. City of Oxford Motor Services Ltd placed 16 on LD3RA chassis with synchromesh gearboxes in service early in 1958 though rather surprisingly they seated only 65 passengers. Seen here is one of the eight bodied by Park Royal. *ACV/Ian Allan Library*

Right:
Home-market demand for double-deckers was sluggish in the later 1950s. Hence major exports were particularly welcome and, remarkably, the Teheran Omnibus Board placed a first order for no less than 250 Regent V D2LA models, delivered in 1958. These had Park Royal bodywork and were almost a mirror image of contemporary home market models, save for the full-

depth opening windows. However, they had the standard 17ft 6in export wheelbase and had A222 11.3-litre engines. *ACV/Ian Allan Library*

Lodekka was evident in the pursuit of such a concept, with drop-centre rear axle to allow the floor level to be lowered. Its development was entrusted to Crossley, and the MB3RA prototype, for Walsall Corporation, appeared on that firm's stand at the 1956 Show. It and a

demonstrator had the AV470 engine, having been planned as 27ft models though completed as 30ft. A series of delays resulted from redesign to suit a larger engine, a move of production to Park Royal on the closure of Crossley's works and a switch from aluminium to steel for the body framing to suit BET preference, so production did not begin until 1958.

Thus the Regent V continued as AEC's main double-decker in terms of numbers built. There was a

Left:
Monocontrol was AEC's name for the direct-acting version of the Wilson-type epicyclic gearbox which generally replaced the preselective option from the mid-1950s. Movement of the miniature gear lever, actually an electrical switch supplied by CAV, operated the desired change of gear immediately, there being no clutch or gear-change pedal. This view also shows the style of steering wheel and instrument panel of standard AEC passenger models of the period. *CAV/Ian Allan Library*

Below:
The Bridgemaster represented a third strand to AEC ideas on double-deckers. The basic idea of an integral body with the mechanical units in sub-frames and the use of independent front suspension was common to the Routemaster but there were major differences in both mechanical and structural design. Seen here at Park Royal are two part-completed examples, nearest the camera being B3RA137 which entered service as Leicester Corporation No 217 in 1961. Visible in the background are left-hand Regent V chassis for Baghdad and completed Routemasters. *Author's collection*

further increase in the maximum permitted length for two-axle double-deckers to 30ft in 1956, AEC offering the LD2RA and LD3RA to suit. This helped to put the emphasis back towards the 9.6-litre engine, the AV470 being confined to 27ft models.

Home sales of such buses were fairly low at that time but fortunately for AEC there was an expansion of interest in export left-hand-drive double-deckers, the Regent V being also offered in this form, type D2LA, its left-hand A217 engine maintaining AEC's reputation for good accessibility for servicing. The CCFL fleet in Lisbon continued to be a regular customer and, in Iraq, Baghdad took two batches of 100 Regal IIIs from 1951 but swung to double-deckers, with 180 D2LAs in 1958-61. A noteworthy first order from Teheran, Iran, was for 250 D2LAs supplied in 1958.

In late 1958 the heavier goods range was brought up to date with the Mark V models. These had a new pair of engines, still of 9.6- and 11.3-litre capacity (the latter of growing importance as the need for more power grew) but of wet-liner type and designated AV590 and AV690 respectively. More obvious was the new external design with a restyled cab of smooth profile, the front axle being set back to allow entry via a step ahead of it. The Mandator V was designated G4RA and the Mammoth Major V were G6RA or G8RA, with suffix letters to indicate the type of rear bogie fitted — eg G8RAS had single-axle drive, and G6RAW or G8RAW had double-drive using worm-drive axles. The Mammoth Major eight-wheeler continued to be the biggest seller, with 3,116 of

the G8RA variants built in the period to December 1964, though the Mandator G4RA was not too far behind at 2,112, many of these being tractive units for articulated vehicles.

The Mark III goods models were not yet dead, however, and in addition to left-hand versions which continued into the early 1960s there were other exceptions, notably the Mammoth Major six-wheeler increasingly favoured for site work, this being developed as model 3673M with squared cab outline and the type name Dumptruk, of which 579 were built from 1958 to December 1963. This line of thought was taken much further with the 1100 Dumptruk, an altogether bigger machine of bonneted layout and having a new engine, the largest ever produced by AEC, of some 18-litre capacity and called the AV1100. It was also built in horizontal form for railcar applications.

The AV590 engine was also adopted for the 9.6-litre

double-deck range, except for left-hand models and the first production Routemaster (RM8), a Bridgemaster (now designated B3RA) for Sheffield and a Regent V for East Kent so powered being at the 1958 Show. At first, 30ft Regents with the AV590 became 2LD3RA etc, but almost immediately it was decided to drop the L prefix signifying the 30ft length, such buses simply becoming 2D3RA regardless of length. The Bridgemaster went through further variations, including a forward-entrance version, type 2B3RA, and modest numbers were sold, mainly to BET companies, but only 179 had been completed when the model was dropped in 1962.

By no means all double-decker operators favoured the 30ft length at that stage, most notably London Transport with the standard production Routemaster, which was 27ft 6½in long. The unladen weight was 7 tons 5cwt, which was 5cwt less than the standard RT despite seating eight more passengers and being 8ft wide as well as slightly longer. AEC supplied the running gear in the form of the front and rear sub-frames, these being given 'chassis' numbers beginning at R2RH001, the H in the designation signifying the power-hydraulic brake system. The initial order for 850 was soon increased to 2,000. In practice, there were variations, including an initial batch of 24 of a 30ft version designated RML, delivered in 1961-2.

Above:

The Reliance was the most widely favoured underfloor-engined coach chassis on the British market in the late 1950s, chosen by major company groups as well as many independent concerns. Greenslades Tours Ltd of Exeter had come under BET group ownership in 1953, this Reliance MU3RV with Duple Britannia 41-seat bodywork being one of four entering service in the spring of 1958. There were 44 Reliances in this fleet by 1964, more than half the total. *ACV/Ian Allan Library*

Below:

The new Mark V heavy-duty goods range with wet-liner AV590 and AV690 engines appeared in the autumn of 1958, readily identifiable by the set-back front axle, allowing the entrance step to the cab to be ahead of it. The cab was of well-rounded outline, differing from others using the same grille outline in having gently curved lines with no break at waist level. A slight fall in the roof-line from front to rear was another distinctive feature. The Mandator G4RA tractive unit had a very short wheelbase of 8ft 1in — this example is seen coupled to a Scammell semi-trailer. *AEC/Ian Allan Library*

Above:

This view of the same vehicle shows how the layout of the Mark V goods models gave relatively easy cab entry for the driver. *AEC/Ian Allan Library*

Top:
Routemaster production got under way for London Transport late in 1958, most of those built in the early years being used for trolleybus replacement. The standard RM had the AV590 engine, automatic gearbox, power-assisted steering, seated 64 and weighed a modest 7 tons 5cwt. Seen lined up in the former trolleybus depot at Hanwell are five examples used to replace the 607 and 655 trolleybus routes in November 1960.
Ian Allan Library

Above:
The largest models in the Dumptruk range and in most respects the biggest AECs of all were the 1100 series with 18-litre AV1100 engine, of which the basic model HDK4LA was introduced in 1959. Seventy had been built by 1962. Here one makes a standard London RT look quite small.
AEC/Ian Allan Library

10. Take-Over…and Decline

Exports were regarded as the key to expansion by the beginning of the 1960s, some efforts proving more successful than others. A new bonneted goods range mechanically equivalent to the forward control Mark V types, but with a wide angular radiator lacking the triangle badge, had been announced in 1959. The Mogul GB4LA was two-axle and the Majestic GB6RA or GB6LA was three-axle; overall, 132 had been built in the next five years. The heavier-duty Super Mammoth HG6RAB, using the 18-litre AV1100 engine, was a more specialist machine, with 73 produced over the 1961-4 period.

Local assembly plants were set up in Belgium, Holland and Portugal in 1960 in conjunction with local firms to add to those already in existence. That year the Regal

Below:
A link with the Dutch bodybuilding concern Verheul resulted in the building of this demonstrator ACLO Regal IV aimed at the South American market in the latter part of 1959. Almost identical bodywork was chosen for 150 vehicles on the Regal VI model U2LA chassis with AH690 engine for service in Montevideo, Uruguay, delivery of which began in 1962 — similar buses were also supplied to Lima, Peru. *AEC/Ian Allan Library*

Mark VI was announced as an export-only successor to the Regal Mark IV, using an AH690 wet-liner engine, available with Monocontrol epicyclic or a six-speed synchromesh gearbox, the latter another sign of the times in being a bought-out unit from the German ZF concern. Chassis were designated U2RA, U2LA etc, and again the left-hand versions proved the more popular — some 500 were supplied to Buenos Aires, Argentina, and nearly 1,000 had been built by the end of 1964, plus just over 300 right-hand models.

For South Africa, a special bus model called the Kudu was assembled locally, with AV690 vertical engine mounted at the front — this being considered preferable on dirt roads — yet retaining the entrance ahead of the front axle. A simpler front-engined bus — basically a Mercury adapted for passenger work — was given the name Ranger and had been in production since 1957. Some 556 had been built by the end of 1964, in this case at first mainly M4RA right-hand models, though 174 of this figure were M4LA with left-hand steering, a number that was to grow over the years — later versions were built right through to 1979.

Above:
The Regal VI also had quite a strong following in Australia. One operated by the Metropolitan Transport Trust in Perth, Western Australia, is seen in December 1984 in company with some of the Mercedes-Benz O305 buses which had become standard by then. *Nicholas Pusenjak*

Below:
This example of a typical Mercury of the time was owned by CAV Ltd, being seen in 1961 leaving the firm's works in Rochester bound for the factory of the firm's French associate Roto Diesel, in Blois. *CAV/Ian Allan Library*

Above:
What proved to be an important addition to the range for 1962 was the Marshal GM6RH, a medium-weight six-wheeler variant with 20-ton gross vehicle weight rating using the AV470 engine and other Mercury range units — by that date the five-speed gearbox was of constant-mesh instead of synchromesh type. Seen here in the works drive is an example of the GM6RHS single-axle-drive version being used for a road test by *Modern Transport*, published in June 1962. *Ian Allan Library*

Right:
British Road Services was a major user of AEC goods vehicles during the period of its existence as part of the state-owned sector. This modified version of the Mark V cab with the windscreen panels in flat glass was introduced to meet its requirements, seen here on a Mandator G4RA tractive unit of 1961. *AEC/Ian Allan Library*

In 1961, Thornycroft was added to the ACV group, and although only specialist vehicles remained in production, its Basingstoke factory subsequently took on a new role as, in effect, AEC's gearbox factory, while the Maudslay works was similarly turned over to axle manufacture.

Export competition was becoming stronger from such European firms as Mercedes-Benz and Volvo; Japanese commercial vehicle makers were also beginning to grow in importance. The idea that it might be better for Leyland and AEC to join forces to compete abroad more effectively led to a proposal for what was called a merger of the Leyland and ACV groups, announced at a press conference on 5 June 1962. I was by then a transport journalist and was present on that historic occasion — I still recall my sense of foreboding at the long-term implications for AEC, despite the upbeat presentation — the choice of Leyland Motor Corporation as the title was an indication of the true position.

Ironically, London Transport had elected to have Leyland O.600 engines in some of its Routemasters

Top:
The increase in permitted length to 36ft led to the introduction of new versions of the Reliance to suit. The Oxford fleet took delivery of eight of the Reliance 470 type to the new length with Marshall 53-seat bodywork in 1962. Four of them, including 772 seen here, were of 4MU3RA type with synchromesh gearboxes. A forward-entrance Bridgemaster is also visible. *G. W. Fisk*

Above:
Scottish Omnibuses Ltd was also a user of the Reliance in 4MU3RA form in the earlier 1960s, though switching to the AH590-engined 2U3RA version in 1966. Seen leaving St Andrew's Square bus station for Galashiels is B921, new in August 1963 and having an early example of the Alexander Y-type body widely favoured by the Scottish Bus Group. *AEC/Ian Allan Library*

Above:

The Renown low-floor double-deck model replaced the Bridgemaster, using a conventional chassis but designed to allow forward-entrance layout with one step up from ground to floor level. This view of chassis 3B3RA008 for the South Wales fleet when ready for delivery to the bodybuilders, also shows the drop-centre rear axle allowing the low floor level to continue to the rear of the bus. *AEC/Ian Allan Library*

Below:

Sister Renown chassis 3B3RA007 is seen here after receiving its Park Royal 71-seat body and entering service in 1963 — there were a total of 14 similar buses plus five with Willowbrook bodywork in that year's delivery to the South Wales fleet. The Renown's front end differed from that of the Bridgemaster in that the offside mudguard projected slightly at the foot of the cab front panel. *AEC/Ian Allan Library*

Top:
The London Brick Co Ltd had been a regular operator of AEC
vehicles since the 1930s, the Mammoth Major being a
favoured type over that period. This Mark V example of 1963
had a cab of non-standard outline in moulded plastics by Road
Transport Services (Hackney) Ltd, having rear-hinged doors
and flat-glass windscreens. The body used expanded metal in
the dropside panels. *AEC/Ian Allan Library*

Above:
At first the Mark V forward-control goods range was not offered
in left-hand-drive form, there being no left-hand version of the
AV590 or AV690 engine, and the left-hand Mark III goods
models continued for a time. This Mammoth Major Mark V six-
wheeler with transparent plastic cab fitted for display purposes
was among the limited number of exceptions.
AEC/Ian Allan Library

following trials in 1961, to avoid AEC having too much of an monopoly position. There was considerable annoyance among LT's engineers when news of the merger came through but the scheme went ahead, 573 more such engines being fitted to buses delivered in 1962-4.

Yet it took time for consequences of the take-over to become evident. AEC had just introduced new versions of the Reliance to suit the increase in maximum length for two-axle single-deckers operating in Britain from 30ft to 36ft (11m) which came into effect in 1961. One, the Reliance 470, had the same AH470 engine as existing versions but the other, more important in its implications, was the Reliance 590, using the AH590 engine and ZF six-speed synchromesh gearbox, type 2U3RA. It was the first British-built coach on the market to be able to take full advantage of the new motorways by being able to cruise at an unfussed 70mph. Reliance models of broadly similar types were to form a substantial part of AEC output until the end of production. Air suspension began to

be available on underfloor-engined models, the Regal VI then becoming 3U3RA etc and, more rarely, the Reliance 4U3RA etc.

A new Renown model, the third to bear the name, was a low-height front-engined double-decker to replace the Bridgemaster, a market that seemed to fascinate makers despite modest sales. The factory was already committed to build it before the merger, otherwise it would probably have been abandoned — a directly equivalent Leyland/Albion model, the Lowlander, had been introduced the previous year. The Renown reverted to a separate chassis (to allow a choice of bodybuilder) and a beam front axle with leaf springs, though air suspension was used at the rear. It retained the front-mounted AV590 engine and could have either a synchromesh or epicyclic gearbox (this latter not available on the Bridgemaster), being designated 3B3RA or 3B2RA accordingly.

The Renown was a well-thought out example of its type, its frame allowing the provision of a spacious single-step entrance. Yet in comparative trials against the Leyland Atlantean and Daimler Fleetline, introduced in 1958 and 1960 respectively and both with rear-engined layout, it seemed old-fashioned. The half-cab frontal appearance was much the same as the Regent V and the gearbox of the synchromesh version was noisy. Sales were

Above:
The Carris (Lisbon Electric Tramways) concern continued to add to its fleet of left-hand Regent V models up to 1966. As well as 213 on chassis supplied from Southall from 1957 onwards, there were 57 to LD2RA specification supplied in unit form in 1964-5 and completed as integral double-deckers by UTIC, by then a regular builder of integral buses and coaches using AEC mechanical units. They had A222 11.3-litre 'left-hand' engines and Monocontrol transmission. The two seen here arriving at the Cais do Sodre terminus in Lisbon retain the characteristic look of AEC chassis and Weymann bodywork of earlier examples. *Phil Trotter*

again disappointing — the market for such buses was limited — and by 1965 it had been decided to drop the model — 251 were built, the last delivered in 1967. Ironically, most were synchromesh and had Park Royal bodies, going largely to BET fleets.

The first outward signs of the effects of the merger came in 1964, when the Ergomatic tilt cab designed by Leyland was introduced and adopted across most of the LMC group's forward-control goods range including those of AEC as well as Leyland and Albion, giving an impression of standardisation, although the mechanical design of the new AEC range, which retained the familiar names and form of designation but now with a 'T' prefix, was still that of true AEC products. As well as conforming to contemporary styling trends, the new cab was more 'civilised' and quieter internally but proved prone to rusting.

There was a revised engine range, reverting to 'dry' cylinder liners in place of the wet cylinder liners (in direct contact with the cooling water) that had been favoured from the mid to late 1950s but which proved prone to gasket trouble — the AV471 and AV691 directly replacing the AV470 and AV690, etc. There were also new engine sizes, the AV505 and AH505 being derived from the 470 but with 116mm bore and of 8.2-litre capacity. The Reliance switched to the AH505 (the chassis designations then becoming 6MU3R etc) or AH691, in which case the designations were 6U3ZR etc, though chassis with air suspension became 8U. At the end of 1967, AEC became the first maker to offer 12m passenger models for use in Britain after this length became legal, the Reliance 691 becoming available in this form.

The AV760 engine was similarly derived from the 690 but with bore increased to 136mm, making the capacity 12.4 litres and giving a power output of up to 226bhp at 2,200rpm — there was increasing need for more power for the larger goods models then coming into wider favour —

Above:
Bonneted AEC models lost their traditional look in the 1960s, adopting wider styles of bonnet. This Dumptruk 10cu yd model with Edbro tipping body had a 'rugged' version with angular mudguards and also used a cab with reverse-rake windscreen. *AEC/Ian Allan Library*

Below:
Articulated vehicles were becoming increasingly common for heavier-duty goods applications. This late example of a Mandator V tractive unit dating from 1965 and operated by Esso is seen coupled to a 4,120gal tanker semi-trailer. The stainless steel tank, designed to carry liquefied ethylene gas, was by Butterfield. *Esso/Ian Allan Library*

at that date it was among the largest British engines intended for general use in haulage vehicles. An early application for the AV760 was a new pair of Militant 6x6 models, type O870 and O880, the latter with left-hand steering, for gross weights of 28 tons or gross train weights of up to 56 tons. In addition to military applications, they were offered for general sale from 1966 — respectively, 300 and 311 were built.

Another aspect of group co-ordination was seen in new rear-engined single-deckers also announced in 1964. The frame structure, allowing a low floor line except at the rear, was common between Leyland's Panther and AEC's Swift models, although the respective engines and other units were of the respective makers' designs. What was intended to be the standard Swift had the AH505, though a heavier-duty model using the AH691 was at first called the Merlin, this name being adopted by London Transport even though before production began AEC decided to call

Left:
The first clear evidence of AEC's merger with the Leyland Motor Corporation was the introduction of the Ergomatic cab for most of the group's major goods ranges in time for the 1964 Show. The concept of a tilting cab had come from America, but this extended its use considerably in Britain. The degree of access to the AV691 or AV760 engine fitted to the Mandator or Mammoth Major models is evident in this view. The characteristic AEC style of wheel hub continued, indicating the retention of the marque's own chassis design.
AEC/Ian Allan Library

Below:
The Ergomatic cab was of basically uniform design across the group, the various marques being distinguished only by badges and minor details, though the chassis designs continued to differ considerably. Here a 1966 Mandator with semi-trailer of Meacher's Transport Ltd of Southampton is posed alongside one of Cunard's prewar 'Queen' liners, then nearing the end of their working lives, at Southampton docks. *AEC/Ian Allan Library*

Top:
The Swift rear-engined single-decker was also introduced in 1964, one of the first examples being this demonstrator with Willowbrook 53-seat body — the author carried out a road test of it for Bus & Coach magazine in 1965. It was an MP2R model with the AH505 8.2-litre engine set to give 149bhp and Monocontrol gearbox. It went well and was quite light on fuel, the only adverse recollection being of rather heavy steering. As part of an effort to standardise components with Leyland it did not have AEC's worm and nut system, usually good in this respect. *AEC/Author's collection*

Above:
Production of the Routemaster continued, almost exclusively for London Transport. Versions for Green Line commuter services were introduced, the second batch built in 1965 being of 30ft length and having comfortable seats for 65 passengers. Seen here on test by AEC before being handed over for service is RCL2224. *AEC/Ian Allan Library*

Below:

The Regent V was quietly building up to bigger numbers than even the Routemaster. Leeds City Transport had regarded successive types of AEC Regent as its standard buses since the early 1930s, and in 1965-6 received its final batch of 20 of the 2D2RA type with locally built Roe bodywork, the latter also traditional in Leeds. By the early 1960s, standardisation on 8ft width made it possible to use parallel-sided frames which allowed wider spacing of the front springs and a noticeable gain in stability. One of the 1966 deliveries is seen at Gipton in 1974. *C. J. Spring*

Bottom:

The bus that might have opened a fresh chapter in AEC's traditional role as a maker of double-deck buses was the rear-engined Routemaster, retaining all the front-engined model's advanced engineering but in a format more in tune with contemporary demand. There were to have been three, including a demonstrator, at the 1966 Show, with clear indications of wider interest but the project was dropped. Only one was completed, becoming London Transport's FRM1, seen here on sightseeing tour duty at Piccadilly Circus in 1979. *G. K. Kilberry*

Above:
It became permissible for buses and coaches operating in Britain to be up to 12m in length from September 1967 and AEC was the first maker to announce a suitable chassis meeting British regulations. At first, demand was quite small but among early users of the resulting Reliance model was Premier Travel Ltd of Cambridge which took delivery of two early examples with Alexander Y-type 53-seat bodywork early in 1969. The unladen weight nowadays seems very modest at just under 8 tons.
Alexander/Author's collection

the type the Swift 691 for general sale.

A major change in policy caused London to order larger fleets of single-deckers than hitherto — initially 665 Merlins were added to the fleet as its MB class in the period from 1966 to 1969. It was found that 11m single-deckers were too long to negotiate many of the twisty suburban routes, and a switch was made to a 10m version for a further 838, but it was not possible to accomodate the AH691 engine in its reduced overhang and these were thus Swift models with AH505 engine. They formed

Left:
New Construction and Use Regulations of 1964 allowed articulated vehicles to run at 32 tons gross if the weight was carried on five axles spread over an approved distance. This led to a demand for a twin-steering tractor unit, lighter than the traditional double-drive six-wheel unit. The Mammoth Minor name was revived for the resulting new model TG6RF, introduced in 1965 and usually fitted with the 12.4-litre AV760 engine. This 1966 example was in the fleet of James Hemphill Ltd of Glasgow. *AEC/Ian Allan Library*

Centre left:
The Militant O860 was nearing the end of its production run in 1966 but these three late examples were supplied for use in Sudan by the Geological Surveys Department.
AEC/Ian Allan Library

Above right:
What was effectively AEC's swan-song in terms of engine design was the V8 engine introduced in May 1968 as the 'British Leyland 800-series'. Developing 247bhp from a compact 12.154-litre engine without turbocharging was an impressive achievement at the time. However, vee-form engines are notorious for needing careful development if they are to give reliable service, and it seems that not enough was given in this case. *AEC/Ian Allan Library*

Right:
An attractive feature of the V8 Mandator cab was the layout, with engine under the seats, with provision for a centre seat directly over it. The Ergomatic cab was already better than most for its time in terms of comfort and gained further in reduction of noise in this form, as well as allowing the driver to use the nearside door where preferable. This example had an epicyclic gearbox, using the Leyland-style direct pneumatic control. *AEC/Ian Allan Library*

London's SM class, delivery continuing until 1972.

Sadly, these last major London bus classes using AEC chassis were far from successful. The horizontal engines mounted under the rear overhang were combined with fluid flywheels and epicyclic gearboxes into compact assemblies, and this form of construction lacked the free flow of air round the separate units given by the layout used on the Routemaster or Regent models with epicyclic gearboxes. Chronic overheating and seizure problems were suffered in London's increasing traffic congestion. LT engineers also criticised other features, notably the brake equipment, on what they regarded as these 'off the shelf' buses by contrast with earlier types developed jointly by engineers at Chiswick and Southall. On the other hand, some provincial and export users found the Swift suited their needs well.

Meanwhile, AEC's involvement in double-deck bus construction, its mainstream activity from the beginning, was coming to an end. This proved to be among the first major results of the merger and had the effect of curtailing the output of the company. As it turned out, the demand for double-deckers was about to rise, and several hitherto important AEC customers were forced to switch to other makes, usually Daimler or Leyland. Routemaster production had continued steadily until 1966 but then slowed before ending in 1968, when the London Transport

RM class reached its total of 2,760 vehicles. The 30ft-long 72-seat RML had become standard from 1965 with a final 500 buses, preceded by 43 Green Line coach versions of this length. It is a remarkable tribute to its quality that the Routemaster is still a familiar sight in London 30 years after the last examples were built, even if many have been re-engined and refurbished internally.

There had been a very half-hearted effort to sell the model to other operators following the appearance of a 30ft forward-entrance version, RMF1254, at the 1962 Show, but the only such customer was Northern General Transport, then a BET subsidiary, which took a total of 50 broadly similar buses but with Leyland engines in 1964-5. There were also 65 British European Airways Routemaster coaches, also forward-entrance but shorter, in 1966-7, but that concern's coach services and choice of vehicles were still managed by London Transport.

The trend towards rear-engined layout for buses led to a design for a rear-engined version of the Routemaster in which both London Transport and other operators had

expressed interest. There were plans for one to be exhibited in Sheffield Corporation livery at the 1966 Show before Leyland group management killed off the project save for one prototype for London, numbered FRM1, delivered without publicity in June 1966. It had an AV691 engine mounted transversely at the rear and layout akin to other rear-engined models but otherwise retained the advanced specification and many parts from the front-engined versions. In fairness, London Transport had itself undermined the project by indicating that its double-deck needs would be much reduced. In fact, this policy was reversed only about two years later, but the resulting big orders went to Daimler for Fleetline double-deckers.

The Regent V had soldiered on and, despite much of its basic concept still being traceable to RT1 of 1939, it actually outsold even the Routemaster. Some 3,702 Regent V chassis had been built when the last left the factory in 1968, of which 980 were left-hand examples. The design had been developed mildly in the earlier 1960s, standardisation on 8ft width allowing the use of wider-spaced front springs with a significant gain in stability, and from 1966, the 11.3-litre AV691 engine became standard for home-market buses, albeit much derated to 128bhp, barely more than the 9.6 gave if set to produce full power 20 years earlier.

Left:
An additional goods model variant introduced in late 1968 was an eight-wheeled version of the Marshal, catering for up to 24 tons gross. As with most earlier six- or eight-wheeled models, it was available with single- or double-drive and the option of a fully articulated rear bogie for use on rough ground.
Ian Allan Library

In May 1968, a further major merger created the British Leyland Motor Corporation, linking the existing Leyland group, which by then also included Rover and Land-Rover with what was generally known as BMC, incorporating the mass-production car makers, Austin and Morris, as well as the Jaguar-Daimler-Guy group.

Only 10 days later came the announcement of what was called the 'British Leyland 800-series' V8 diesel engine. In fact, this was an AEC design, its origins going back to 1962. The bore size was 130mm and the stroke 114mm, giving a swept volume of 12.154 litres. Although not turbocharged, it gave 247bhp at 2,600rpm in a compact package which fitted under the seats in the Ergomatic cab of the V8 Mandator VTG4R tractive unit for 32-ton-gross articulated vehicles introduced on the same date. Sadly, inadequate development meant that reliability was not satisfactory, and although a rear-engined coach version, the Sabre, appeared at the 1970 Show and a few export Daimler Roadliner buses were so powered, the 800-series V8 was dropped after only three years.

Yet at the beginning of the 1970s, AEC at Southall continued to be a substantial maker of goods and single-deck passenger chassis, still in most respects of its own design. The former were principally the tilt-cab versions of the Mercury, Marshal, Mandator and Mammoth Major with straight-six AEC engines and the latter mainly the Reliance, demand for which remained quite brisk, largely from independent coach operators for whom the six-speed ZF synchromesh option was attractive — at that stage the Leopard was available only with Pneumocyclic semi-automatic transmission.

The Swift was deleted from the home market range as part of a group exercise to build up demand for the Leyland National single-deck bus put into production from 1972 at Whitehaven as a joint venture with the National Bus Company — the latter being the state-owned group resulting from a merger of the former Tilling and BET bus interests in Britain. Yet AEC continued to export the Swift, now with the horizontal AH760 version of the 12.4-litre engine, 65 going to Durban in 1974, for example. The type found a very receptive market in Portugal via UTIC, which regularly took sets of units with ZF gearboxes right up to the end of all production at Southall in 1979.

As home-market Swift orders died away, the Reliance became the only passenger model offered in the UK — over 300 were sold in 1972, though dropping somewhat in later years. The AH760 also became the only engine option for this model from 1973, although with output restricted to 165bhp at 2,000rpm, well down on the 220bhp used in some goods applications.

From January 1972 a new strictly sequential chassis numbering system was introduced, beginning at 21165 and replacing the separate series for each type as used by AEC for half a century, though the model designation prefix codes continued. The new system made total annual output figures more readily apparent — that for 1972 was 3,095, to which 835 chassis produced in 'completely knocked down' form for export could be added. In 1973 there was a rise to 3,992 — in round figures, 80 per week — plus 786 ckd sets of parts. The Southall factory was still a busy place.

However, by the early 1970s, BLMC was beginning to run into financial problems stemming from the Austin-Morris car business and profits from the group's commercial vehicle business were being syphoned off to try and save the car side, all to no avail. The group was only rescued from complete collapse by being taken into State ownership from December 1974. By then, AEC was largely a goods vehicle maker and increasingly regarded

as a satellite of Leyland. The production line had been reorganised to suit the output having become mainly of short-wheelbase tractive units. Output from AEC had begun to decline as work was increasingly concentrated on Leyland's factories in the north of England, falling to around 1,600 chassis built annually in 1976-8, although there were 998 ckd chassis sets in 1976.

Major new design work was all handled at Leyland, and indeed some senior ex-AEC engineering staff had moved there by the mid-1960s, not least Bob Fryars, who had been appointed Chief Engineer of the LMC Truck Division in 1966. AEC influence was also still evident in engine design, for while the new L11 and TL11 series were derived from the Leyland 680, the TL12 was based on the AH760, and even retained the 142mm stroke dimension which had been characteristic of heavier-duty AEC diesel engines right back to the pioneering A155 of 1930, through the various 8.8-, 9.6-, 11.3- and 12.4-litre engines produced over the years. The Leyland Marathon powered by the TL12 was in production at Southall at the end — one of them was the last chassis to come down the line.

The Reliance had retained a loyal if modest home-market following to the end, almost always as a coach chassis, and mainly among independent operators. Even so, when it became known that AEC's future was in doubt, operators tended to look elsewhere for new chassis, and Volvo, in particular, gained substantial ex-AEC business for its B58 model. Yet it was fitting that among the last deliveries still being made (after bodying at Duple or Plaxton) as the factory closed were 90 of the 6U2R type for Green Line service, by then being run by London Country Bus Services Ltd, part of the National Bus Company.

Above:
The Marshal six-wheeler was to prove one of AEC's most popular models in the later years. These two short-wheelbase examples with tanker bodywork were supplied to King Oil of Norwich. *AEC/Author's collection*

Above right:
The Swift sold in modest numbers outside London, being chosen by several municipal fleets, some finding it well suited to their needs until the model was withdrawn from the home market along with other existing BLMC rear-engined bus models in favour of the Leyland National. Morecambe Corporation had been a regular user of AEC buses since 1932, and in 1970 it placed three Swift models with Northern Counties bodywork in service. *AEC/Author's collection*

Right:
By 1970, the bulk delivery of propane gas to rural farms and households was gaining in popularity, Shell-Mex and BP Gases Ltd having adopted the name Propagas, as displayed on this Mercury tanker. *AEC/Author's collection*

Briefly during 1977-8 it had seemed that Southall might again be involved with double-deckers when plans for Leyland's rear-engined B15, later called Titan, to be transferred from Park Royal were considered but that project fell through and the closure of the factory came on 25 May 1979.

Overall, the dice were loaded against its survival, with no room for expansion — the only space within the site, the sports field, was scheduled as an open space. Perhaps more crucial was a shortage of skilled labour in the area, influenced by the growth of maintenance workshops at London Airport nearby, and consequent high wage rates.

So a once-great enterprise vanished, but its place in transport history is secure.

Right:
Glenton Tours Ltd catered for the top end of the tours market, its discreet image being conveyed by the 'quiet' yet always immaculate metallic fawn livery. One of its distinctive Reliance coaches with a special version of Plaxton's Panorama Elite body having centre-entrance layout is seen here picking up passengers in London for a tour of Denmark.
AEC/Author's collection

Below:
For the last few years of AEC production, the Reliance was the only home-market passenger model, retaining a loyal following to the end. It was a happy coincidence that, as the factory closed in 1979, the Green Line fleet, by then part of London Country Bus Services Ltd, was taking delivery of a fleet of coaches on Reliance 6U2R chassis with either Duple or, as seen here, Plaxton bodywork. The photograph was taken in Paignton in June 1983, the vehicle being on National Express duties.
G. H. F. Atkins